The Complete Chicken Breast Cookbook

Easy and Delicious Everyday Recipes for the Whole Family

Marge Poore

PRIMA PUBLISHING

PRIMA is a trademark of Prima Publishing, a Division of Prima Communications, Inc.

Library of Congress Cataloging-in-Publication Data

Poore, Marge.
    The complete chicken breast cookbook : easy and delicious everyday recipes for the whole faimly / Marge Poore.
       p.   cm.
    Includes index.
    ISBN 0-7615-0005-7
    1. Cookery (Chicken)   I. Title.
TX750.5.C45P66   1995
641.6'65—dc20   95-1605
                                                CIP

95 96 97 98 99 AA 10 9 8 7 6 5 4 3 2 1

Printed in the United States of America

How to Order:
Single copies may be ordered from Prima Publishing, P.O. Box 1260BK, Rocklin, CA 95677; telephone (916) 632-4400. Quantity discounts are also available. On your letterhead, include information concerning the intended use of the books and the number of books you wish to purchase.

Contents

Acknowledgments

Thanks to Dottye Rinefort, Camille Tarantino, Barbara Miller, and Linda Hennen for their meticulous and cheerful help while working with me to test the recipes in this book. Their efforts are greatly appreciated.

Thanks to my husband Bill for his createve ideas, interest, and pride in the cookbook project, and especially for eating lots of chicken and making valuable suggestions during the months of recipe testing.

Introduction & Chicken Basics

Chicken breasts? Oh yes, they are hands-down and across the country the best-selling, most popular meat product of all. Chicken breasts are nutritious, versatile, economical, and easy to prepare, and almost everybody likes them. They are available everywhere, either fresh for immediate use or conveniently frozen for home storage.

There are so many ways to prepare chicken breasts that they can literally be served several times each week without becoming boring or predictable. Just the different methods of cooking alone, such as grilling, sautéing, braising, poaching, baking, or roasting, create variety and distinctive tastes. The versatility of chicken breasts is demonstrated in the four chapters of this book, and most recipes are intended as centerpiece entrees or complete light meals. The recipes also reflect today's eating preferences for full-flavored lighter foods with less fat. Chicken breasts give cooks a head start, because they take to seasonings of all kinds and they are truly lowfat. Even when a pat of butter or a small amount of cream is added, the total fat per serving is moderate and the flavor of the finished dish is not compromised.

Boneless breast halves are the most popular cut of the chicken, and they are perfect for quick cooking. In these pages, many enticing recipes use boneless breasts in unusual and exciting ways. Chicken breast tenderloins, called "tenders," are also very popular and are especially useful for sandwiches and salads. There are also recipes for dishes that are at their succulent best when chicken is cooked on the bone with the skin. The bones and skin seal in juices and lend flavor. Every recipe considers the type of chicken breast, method of preparation, and timing instructions to obtain the best results, whether starting with fresh or frozen chicken.

Chicken breasts are always in vogue. No wonder good cooks rely on them for fail-safe meals. Whatever trends come and go, chicken breasts can change costume in a flash, and nearly every food fashion and presentation fits in with the mild, lean meat. Chicken breasts can take bold and new combinations of seasonings and marinades, or they can remain true to traditional sauces, so explore all the possibilities among the delicious recipes in this book, and you'll create plenty of tender and appealing chicken dishes in dozens of guises.

CHICKEN BASICS: Buying, Storing, Thawing, and Cooking

Buying and Storing

High-quality fresh chicken is wonderful, and to ensure that you are purchasing the best, be a fussy consumer. When shopping for fresh chicken breasts, look for smooth, moist, unbruised skin, or if skinless, a moist, fresh look with little or no juices in the tray. Avoid torn packages, and check the sell date on the package. Fresh chicken should not have any "off-putting" odors. Remember that chicken is susceptible to harmful bacteria that grows at warm temperatures, so follow a few simple rules for utmost safety. Keep it cold, buy it last, and store it in the refrigerator as soon as you reach home. For extended shopping outings it's a good idea to carry a small cooler and ice-pack in the car to keep chicken cold for temporary storage. Use fresh chicken breasts within two days of purchase, or freeze them at once in airtight freezer bags if you're planning to use them later. Recommended storage time in the freezer is four months.

Commercially frozen chicken breasts are extremely popular these days, and they are widely available in major supermarkets and warehouse stores. Although many professional cooks and chefs prefer fresh and believe it to be superior, with better flavor than frozen, the public apparently believes otherwise, and sales continue to climb for this convenient and economical product. Freezing techniques have advanced, and today's quickly frozen chicken breasts may actually be fresher than some of the packaged fresh chicken, which sits for several days in the market. Properly frozen chicken breasts are an excellent product and a real boon for today's cooks whose schedules are often hectic and unpredictable.

Purchasing chicken parts is both convenient and economical, and chicken breasts are available in several cuts. Consumers can choose from fresh whole breasts with bones and skins, or whole boneless breasts with skins. There are also fresh half-breasts with skins and rib bones, or boneless half-breasts with skins. Chicken breast tenders, which are individual fillet strips, are the newest of the individual chicken breast pieces now being offered in many stores. Most of these cuts are also available packaged individually in the frozen form.

Individually quick-frozen chicken breast pieces are by far the most popular frozen poultry item on the market. Each breast piece is sealed in an ice glaze to keep it separate from the others. It's easy to pull out the number of pieces needed and leave the rest frozen. Consumers can choose either skinless, boneless breast halves, or breasts with ribs attached, or chicken breast tenders. The package contains helpful information for safe handling, defrosting, and cooking. This cookbook gives directions in each recipe as to the way I prefer to thaw and use frozen chicken breasts. During months of testing, both fresh and frozen chicken breasts were used, and both gave excellent results. Impeccably fresh high-quality chicken breasts are truly delicious, and I choose them when I can, but the quality of the packaged frozen breasts makes it easy to recommend them, too. I will continue to use them often, as my schedule, just like yours, can be unpredictable.

Thawing

The following tested ways to thaw frozen chicken breasts safely are recommended.

1. Whenever possible, thaw chicken breasts overnight in the refrigerator to retain the most juices. When you are ready to start cooking, recipe preparation is even quicker if the chicken breasts are already thawed.

2. Frozen chicken breasts can also be thawed in a microwave. Take care when thawing in the microwave as the delicate edges of the chicken can begin to "cook" before thawing is completed. Power levels and timing can vary for different microwave makes and models. It's best to consult the instruction booklet for your particular microwave.

3. Another method is to place frozen chicken breast halves in a sealed plastic bag (ideally, no more than two pieces in each bag), and place the bag in a large pan of cold tap water. The breasts will become flexible and ready to use in about 35 minutes. To thaw more evenly, turn the bag over occasionally and add fresh tap water once or twice.

4. The quickest method to thaw frozen chicken breasts is to rinse them, individually and directly, under cold, running tap water until they become flexible, which takes about 5 minutes for each breast. Blot with paper towels and proceed with the recipe.

5. To thaw chicken breast tenders, use any of the above methods. The tenders will thaw in less time because of their size.

Cooking

Chicken breasts can be cooked in a variety of ways which are described in the recipes in this cookbook, but the meat should always be well cooked to meet recommended safety standards for poultry. The cooked meat should be white throughout with no visible pink. To test doneness, pierce the thickest part of the meat with the tip of a sharp knife. The juices should run clear. If testing doneness with a meat thermometer, bone-in parts should register a temperature of 170°F and boneless parts should reach a temperature of 160°F. Because chicken breast meat is delicate and cooks quickly, careful attention is needed to avoid overcooking, when the meat can become tough and dry. Certain cooking methods call for the chicken to be browned in fat such as olive oil, vegetable oil, or butter. Fats serve a purpose. They help to keep the meat moist and juicy and aid in the browning. In this book the amount of fat used has been carefully considered and is kept to a minimum.

Keep poultry safety guidelines in mind every time you prepare one of the recipes. It's a known fact that some food products contain harmful bacteria that might cause serious illness if mishandled or cooked improperly. These few safety tips should be followed. Keep chicken refrigerated or frozen until ready to use. Thaw in the refrigerator, microwave, or quickly in cold water. Keep raw poultry separate from all other foods. Wash all working surfaces and utensils well with hot water and soap. Rinse well. Wash hands with hot water and soap after handling raw poultry. Cook chicken thoroughly, and keep hot foods hot and cold foods cold. Refrigerate leftovers right away or throw them away.

No special kitchen equipment is needed to cook the recipes in this book, but heavy-bottomed pans produce the best results and make cooking much easier. Good heavy pans help prevent sticking or burning. I'm a great fan of today's high-quality non-stick surfaces, which are safe, long-wearing, and terrific for chicken cookery. Nonstick frying pans are highly recommended and allow the use of much less fat in the recipes, which lets us create healthier dishes for today's preferred eating patterns.

Another very useful item is the stove-top ridged grill pan. The old-fashioned cast-iron grill pan has been loved for generations for its even heating and excellent heat retention. Ridged grill pans also give those wonderful and appetizing brown grill marks to the cooked surface. Newer-style stove-top grill pans are also available with nonstick surfaces. Recipes that call for chicken breasts to be cooked over coals on an outdoor grill can be cooked in a grill pan equally well.

Cooking chicken is easy and fun, and it produces a multitude of delicious meals. When you explore the chapters and the recipes in this book and start cooking chicken breasts even more often than you already do, no one will complain. Family members and friends may wonder how you come up with such variety from just one cut of chicken, and you'll be rewarded by their anticipation and appreciation whenever chicken is on the menu at your house. Chicken breasts? Oh my, yes! They are wonderful.

1

Superstar Salads and Sandwiches

It's amazing how many unique, sensational salads and sandwiches can be made using chicken breasts as the main ingredient. Their versatility makes wonderful eating, and this chapter contains recipes for chicken salads and sandwiches that serve as satisfying, complete meals. Some are perfect for those who prefer to eat lighter lowfat foods, and others are more hearty and substantial, but all of the dishes here have great color, texture, and flavor. The recipes are easy to follow, and every recipe explains the most practical preparation using either fresh or frozen chicken breasts, so that even those cooks with limited time can enjoy these exciting salads and sandwiches without spending hours in the kitchen.

Salads have come a long way from a chunk of lettuce drizzled with predictable dressings, and today salads really do have superstar status. A greater variety of fresh produce is now available almost everywhere, and taste buds have been awakened by the creative combinations offered by today's adventurous chefs and the glorious photos in cooking publications. The entree salad, hot or cold, has become mainstream, and chicken breasts star when combined with any number of fresh ingredients. The refreshing, crunchy salads in this chapter will brighten any luncheon or light meal.

Sandwiches, too, have never been better. Not only do they profit from the tremendous variety of fresh ingredients to fill them, but the bread choices and quality of breads have reached new heights. Great breads help make great sandwiches, and supermarkets now stock terrific whole-grain breads, sourdough breads, French baguettes, pitas, tortillas, and all sorts of rolls. For sandwiches that are moist, more flavorful and interesting than ever before, there are also condiments galore to slather on the bread, with new ones arriving all the time.

All the hearty chicken breast sandwiches in this chapter will please family members and guests. Most are calorie-controlled, relying on a variety of fillings instead of fat-laden spreads. Chicken breasts and chicken breast tenders are the heart of the sandwiches in this chapter, and you'll want to serve them often.

After trying a number of these scrumptious salads and sandwiches, you may be inspired to create your own variations or invent bold new ones.

Chicken and Chopped Vegetables Sandwich

Diced chicken with a tasty combination of vegetables makes a terrific sandwich that's great for picnics. The filling and bread can be transported separately, and the sandwiches can be assembled on-site. Serve with chips.

3   fresh or frozen skinless, boneless chicken breast halves
1   cup low-salt chicken broth, canned or homemade
      (page 177)
1/2   teaspoon dried oregano, crumbled
1   jar (6 ounces) marinated artichoke hearts, chopped
1/4   cup chopped black olives
1/2   red bell pepper, seeded and chopped
2   green onions, including 2 inches of green, chopped
2   to 3 tablespoons mayonnaise, regular or lowfat
1/2   teaspoon ground cumin
      Freshly ground black pepper
12   slices whole-grain country bread or rye bread
      Lettuce leaves (optional)

1. For fresh chicken, go to step 2. If breasts are frozen, to
   thaw quickly, rinse under cold running water for 3 to 5 minutes or until flexible.

2. Trim fresh or thawed chicken breasts of any visible fat.
   Place breasts in a medium-deep skillet with chicken broth
   and oregano. Bring to a boil over medium heat, then reduce heat to low, cover and cook, turning once until just
   firm to the touch and white throughout, 10 to 12 minutes.
   Remove breasts to a plate. Cover with plastic wrap, and let
   sit about 5 minutes. Cut breasts into small, neatly diced
   pieces. Place in a medium, nonreactive bowl and combine
   with remaining ingredients, except bread and lettuce. Season with freshly ground black pepper.

3. Spread chicken salad generously on 6 bread slices. Add
   lettuce, if desired. Cover with remaining bread slices. Cut in
   half and serve.

Serves 6

Artichoke and Chicken Salad with Red and Yellow Tomatoes

Vine-ripened red and yellow tomatoes add special flavor and color to an inventive chicken entree salad. The tomatoes and baby red new potatoes can usually be found in farmers' markets or specialty produce stores.

Dressing:

3 1/2 tablespoons olive oil
2   tablespoons red wine vinegar
1   teaspoon Dijon mustard
1   tablespoon finely chopped parsley

In a small bowl, whisk dressing ingredients together. Set aside.

Salad:

8   small red new potatoes (about 1 pound), unpeeled, rinsed, and quartered
1   large garlic clove, pressed
1   tablespoon olive oil
       Salt and freshly ground black pepper
4   fresh or frozen skinless, boneless chicken breast halves
1   cup low-salt chicken broth, canned or homemade (page 177)
1   teaspoon dried oregano, crumbled
1   package (9 ounces) frozen artichoke hearts
1   large, ripe, red tomato, cut into bite-size pieces
1   large, ripe, yellow tomato, cut into bite-size pieces
       Salad greens
       Fresh basil sprigs or leaves (optional)

1. Preheat oven to 400°. Place potatoes in a large, ovenproof baking pan. Toss to coat with garlic and olive oil. Sprinkle lightly with salt and pepper. Roast in preheated oven 20 to 25 minutes or until tender. Remove from oven and cool.

2. For fresh chicken, go to step 3. If breasts are frozen, to thaw quickly, rinse under cold running water for 3 to 5 minutes or until flexible.

3. Trim fresh or thawed chicken of any visible fat. Cut each breast into bite-size pieces. Place chicken pieces in a medium saucepan with chicken broth and oregano. Bring to a boil over medium-high heat. Reduce heat to low, cover, and simmer until no longer pink, 5 to 6 minutes. With a slotted spoon, remove chicken pieces to large, nonreactive bowl. Cover and set aside.

4. Strain the broth, return broth to the pan, and cook the artichoke hearts until tender, about 10 to 12 minutes. Drain artichokes by pouring broth through a wire strainer into a bowl, and save broth for another purpose.

5. Put artichoke hearts in the bowl with chicken. Add the roasted potatoes. Whisk the dressing again, and pour over the salad. Toss to coat. Season to taste with salt and pepper. Gently stir in the tomatoes. To serve, divide greens equally among four serving plates. Top greens equally with the chicken salad. Garnish with fresh basil.

Serves 4

Asparagus and Chicken Salad

Fresh asparagus and tender chicken are great salad partners. For a satisfying luncheon or light meal entree, serve the salad with toasted sourdough bread.

1/2	cup mayonnaise, regular or lowfat
1/2	cup plain yogurt, lowfat or regular
1	teaspoon fresh lemon juice
1/2	teaspoon Dijon mustard
1	jar (2 ounces) diced pimientos
1	green onion, white part only, minced
	Freshly ground black pepper
24	asparagus tips
12	fresh or frozen chicken tenders (about 12 ounces)
	Salt
2	tablespoons vegetable oil
	Butter lettuce leaves, washed and dried
4	cherry tomatoes, halved
2	hard-cooked eggs, peeled and quartered

1. In a medium bowl, whisk together until smooth the mayonnaise, yogurt, lemon juice, and mustard. Add pimientos, green onion, and 3 to 4 grinds of pepper. Cover and refrigerate until ready to use.

2. In a large pot of boiling salted water, cook asparagus tips, uncovered, until crisp-tender, about 4 minutes. Drain and cool in a pan of ice water. Drain and pat dry with paper towels. Cover and refrigerate until ready to use.

3. For fresh chicken, go to step 4. If chicken tenders are frozen, place in a sealed plastic bag and thaw in a large pan of cold water about 25 minutes or until flexible. Blot with paper towels.

4. Sprinkle fresh or thawed chicken lightly with salt. In a large, nonstick skillet, heat oil over medium heat and cook tenders, turning, until lightly browned and white throughout, 4 to 5 minutes. Cool on a plate for 6 to 8 minutes, then cut into 1/2-inch pieces. Mix with the mayonnaise dressing.

5. To serve, arrange lettuce leaves on four serving plates. Mound the chicken salad evenly among the plates. Place 6 asparagus tips on each plate, and garnish with tomatoes and hard-cooked eggs.

Serves 4

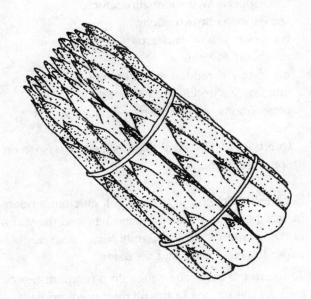

Barbecued Chicken Sandwiches with Cabbage Slaw and Dill Pickles

Healthy whole-meal sandwiches are quick to make, flavorful, and filling. Pass plenty of napkins with these sumptuous juicy sandwiches.

12	fresh or frozen chicken tenders (about 12 ounces)
3	tablespoons olive oil
1	medium onion, halved and thinly sliced
1/2	teaspoon dried oregano, crumbled
1	cup catsup
2	tablespoons Worcestershire sauce
2	tablespoons brown sugar
1	teaspoon yellow mustard
1	teaspoon soy sauce
1/2	cup finely shredded green cabbage
1/2	cup finely shredded red cabbage
2	tablespoons mayonnaise, regular or lowfat
	Salt
2	to 3 baby dill pickles, thinly sliced crosswise on the bias
4	soft sesame buns

1. For fresh chicken, go to step 2. If chicken tenders are frozen, place in a sealed plastic bag and thaw in a large pan of cold water for 25 to 30 minutes or until flexible. Blot with paper towels. Cover and set aside.

2. To make the barbecue sauce, in a medium-heavy saucepan heat 2 tablespoons of the oil over medium heat. Add onion and oregano. Cook, stirring, until onion is limp and translu-

cent, 3 to 4 minutes. Add catsup, Worcestershire sauce, brown sugar, mustard, and soy sauce. Combine and simmer on low heat until thick and shiny, about 3 minutes. Remove from heat.

3. In a medium bowl, combine green and red cabbages with the mayonnaise. Set aside.

4. In a large, nonstick skillet, heat remaining 1 tablespoon of oil over medium heat and add the fresh or thawed chicken tenders. Sprinkle lightly with salt. Cook until lightly browned, about 3 minutes. Turn and cook another 3 minutes, or until firm to the touch and white throughout. Remove to a cutting board and let stand 5 minutes. Cut each tender into 2 or 3 thin strips.

5. To assemble the sandwiches, layer equally the cabbage, barbecue sauce, chicken, and pickles on the bottoms of each bun. Cover with the bun tops and serve.

Serves 4

BLT Chicken Sandwich

Sink your teeth into this terrific combo, which takes the classic BLT a couple steps further by adding chicken and a creamy avocado-chipotle mayonnaise to create a sublime sandwich. Prepared chipotle salsa is available in Mexican specialty shops and many supermarkets. For those who don't relish HOT, leave it out.

4	fresh or frozen skinless, boneless chicken breast halves
1	garlic clove, pressed
1	teaspoon plus 1 tablespoon olive oil
	Salt and freshly ground black pepper
1	large ripe avocado, halved, pitted, and peeled
2	tablespoons mayonnaise, lowfat or regular
1	teaspoon bottled chipotle salsa (optional)
1	teaspoon fresh lime juice
8	slices best-quality whole-grain bread
8	bacon slices, fried until crisp and drained
12	thin tomato slices
1	cup shredded romaine lettuce

1. For fresh chicken, go to step 2. If breasts are frozen, to thaw quickly, rinse under cold running water for 3 to 5 minutes or until flexible.

2. Trim fresh or thawed chicken of any visible fat. Pat dry with paper towels. Rub each breast with garlic and about 1 teaspoon of the olive oil. Sprinkle lightly with salt and pepper. Cut breasts into strips about 1 inch wide. In a large, non-stick skillet, heat 1 tablespoon of oil over medium heat. Add the chicken strips and cook, turning, until lightly browned and white throughout, 3 to 4 minutes total. Set

aside on a plate to cool. When cool enough to handle, tear strips into coarse shreds.

3. In a small bowl, coarsely mash the avocado and combine with mayonnaise, chipotle salsa, and lime juice. Season to taste with salt and pepper.

4. Preheat oven broiler, and lightly toast bread slices on one side. Spread avocado mayonnaise over untoasted sides of each slice. Divide chicken strips equally over 4 of the slices. Top equally with bacon, tomatoes, and lettuce. Cover sandwiches with remaining 4 bread slices. Cut each sandwich in half and serve.

Serves 4

Chicken and Corn Salad with Cumin-Lime Vinaigrette

Corn and tender, shredded chicken make a great cold entree for warm-weather dining. The salad can be made early in the day and assembled shortly before serving.

3	fresh or frozen skinless, boneless chicken breast halves
2	cups low-salt chicken broth, canned or homemade (page 177)
2	ears fresh corn, or 1 1/2 cups frozen corn kernels, thawed
1/2	red bell pepper, finely diced
2	pickled jalapeño chiles, seeded and finely chopped
1	tablespoon minced red onion
3	tablespoons unseasoned rice vinegar
2	tablespoons fresh lime juice
1	tablespoon chopped fresh cilantro or parsley
1	teaspoon ground cumin
1/4	teaspoon sugar
1/4	cup olive oil
	Salt and pepper
	Shredded lettuce

1. For fresh chicken breasts, go to step 2. If breasts are frozen, place in sealed plastic bag and thaw in a large pan of cold water for about 35 minutes or until flexible.

2. Trim fresh or thawed breasts of any visible fat. Place in a medium pan with the chicken broth. Bring to a boil over medium heat, then reduce heat to low, cover, and simmer for about 15 minutes or until meat is white throughout.

Remove breasts to a plate and cover with plastic wrap until cool enough to handle. (Save broth for another use.) With fingers, pull the chicken apart into shreds. Place in a large bowl, and set aside.

3. In a large pan of boiling water, cook the ears of corn for 3 minutes. Drain, cool, and cut kernels away from the cobs. For thawed frozen corn, cook 1 minute in boiling water, then drain in a sieve and cool under running water. Shake sieve of excess water. Place corn in the bowl with the chicken. Add the remaining ingredients except lettuce. Toss together to coat with the dressing. If made ahead, cover and refrigerate until shortly before serving. Serve the salad over a bed of shredded lettuce.

Serves 4

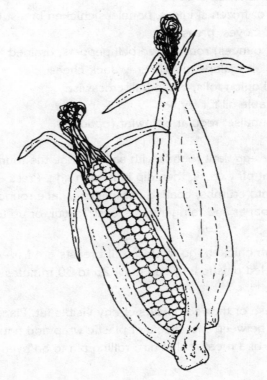

Chicken and Eggplant Sandwiches

These are serious sandwiches for hearty appetites, and they are so good they can become addictive. French fries or chips are good accompaniments.

4	round slices (1/2-inch thick) from a large eggplant
	Salt
1/3	cup flour
1	well-beaten egg
1/3	cup fine bread crumbs
4	fresh or frozen skinless, boneless chicken breast halves
2	garlic cloves, pressed
1	jar (7 ounces) roasted red bell peppers, drained
8	thin slices jalapeño Monterey Jack cheese
4	round onion rolls, cut in half crosswise
	Vegetable oil for frying
	Mayonnaise, regular or lowfat (optional)

1. Sprinkle eggplant rounds with salt. Dredge the rounds in flour, pat off excess, then dip in beaten egg. Press each round into crumbs, coating completely. Place rounds on waxed paper and refrigerate at least 1 hour, or up to 6 hours.

2. For fresh chicken, go to step 3. If breasts are frozen, place in a sealed plastic bag and thaw 25 to 30 minutes or until flexible.

3. Trim fresh or thawed breasts of any visible fat. Place breasts between two sheets of plastic wrap and pound with flat side of a meat mallet or a rolling pin to an even thick-

ness of $1/4$ inch. Sprinkle breasts with salt and rub with garlic. Set aside.

4. Cut roasted peppers into $1/2$-inch strips and place in a bowl. Put sliced cheese on a plate. Put split rolls on a baking sheet, cut sides up. Set all aside.

5. Shortly before serving, line a baking sheet with paper towels. Heat about $1/2$ inch oil in a large, nonstick skillet over medium-high heat. When oil shimmers, add eggplant rounds to hot oil and fry 2 to 3 minutes or until golden brown. Turn and brown other side for 2 to 3 minutes. Drain on paper towels. Keep warm. Pour oil from skillet, wipe skillet with paper towels, and heat 2 tablespoons oil over medium heat. Add chicken breasts and cook, turning, until lightly browned and white throughout but still juicy, 6 to 8 minutes total. Transfer to a plate. Under oven broiler, toast cut side of rolls until barely brown. Place a chicken breast on bottom half of each roll. Put 2 cheese slices on top of each chicken breast, and eggplant rounds on top of cheese. Top equally with red pepper strips. Close sandwiches with roll tops. Serve with mayonnaise, if desired.

Serves 4

Chicken Niçoise Salad

Chicken takes the place of the traditional tuna in this version of niçoise salad, dressed with basil vinaigrette, that's a sure appetite pleaser after a long, hot day.

Basil Vinaigrette:
1   garlic clove, pressed
3   tablespoons red wine vinegar
1/2   teaspoon Dijon mustard
1/2   cup extra virgin olive oil
2   tablespoons chopped fresh basil
      Salt and freshly ground black pepper

In a small bowl, crush the garlic with the vinegar and mustard. Whisk in the oil, pouring it slowly while whisking. Stir in basil. Season to taste with salt and pepper. Set aside.

Chicken Salad:
4   fresh or frozen, skinless, boneless chicken breast halves
      Salt and pepper
2   tablespoons olive oil
1/2   pound small, fresh green beans
6   small new potatoes, washed, with skins on
1   red or yellow bell pepper, seeded and cut into thin strips, 1 1/2 inches by 1/4 inch
2   medium ripe tomatoes, cut into wedges
2   hard-cooked eggs, peeled and quartered
12   niçoise olives
4   anchovy fillets (optional)

1. For fresh chicken, go to step 2. If breasts are frozen, place in a sealed plastic bag and thaw in a large pan of cold water for about 35 minutes or until flexible.

2. Trim fresh or thawed breasts of any visible fat. Sprinkle with salt and pepper. In a large, nonstick skillet, heat oil over medium heat. When oil shimmers, add chicken breasts and cook, turning frequently, until lightly browned and white throughout, 6 to 8 minutes. Remove breasts to a plate and let cool for 10 minutes, then cut crosswise into 1/2-inch strips. Set aside on a plate.

3. Meanwhile, bring a medium pan of salted water to a boil. Cook green beans until crisp-tender, 3 to 4 minutes. With a slotted spoon, remove beans to bowl and cool under cold running water. Drain and set aside. In the same pan of boiling water, cook potatoes until tender, 8 to 10 minutes. With a slotted spoon, remove potatoes from boiling water. Cool under running water, drain, and cut into quarters. Set aside in a separate bowl. In the same water, cook pepper strips for 30 seconds. Cool under running water. Drain and set aside in a separate small bowl. Put tomatoes in another separate bowl.

4. To assemble, toss vegetables separately with about 1 tablespoon of vinaigrette. On a large platter, arrange vegetables, separately, in an attractive pattern, with the chicken mounded in the center. Arrange eggs, olives, and anchovies at random. Drizzle any remaining dressing over the salad. Serve as soon as assembled, or cover and refrigerate for up to 3 hours for best flavor and texture.

Serves 4

Chicken and Quinoa Salad with Snow Peas, Mint, and Cilantro

Quinoa is known as the grain of the Incas. This ancient grain has been rediscovered and has become popular with creative chefs and up-to-the-minute cooks. The best place to buy quinoa is in a health food store. The tiny seeds taste nutty with a very slight bitterness. Toasting in a dry skillet before cooking enhances the nutty flavor.

3	fresh or frozen skinless, boneless chicken breast halves
1	cup quinoa
1/4	teaspoon salt
1/2	cup golden raisins
1/4	cup dried currants
4	tablespoons olive oil
1/2	medium red bell pepper, finely diced
1/4	pound small snow peas, blanched and cut diagonally into 1/2-inch pieces
2	jalapeño chiles, seeded and finely chopped
1/2	teaspoon ground cumin
2	tablespoons fresh lemon juice
1	tablespoon finely chopped fresh mint
1	tablespoon chopped fresh cilantro (fresh basil is good, too)
1/4	cup toasted pine nuts
	Salt and pepper

1. For fresh chicken, go to step 2. If breasts are frozen, place in a sealed plastic bag and thaw in a large pan of cold water for 25 to 30 minutes or until flexible.

2. Trim fresh or thawed chicken of any visible fat. Cut on an angle into strips 1 inch wide. Cover and refrigerate until ready to cook.

3. In a dry, medium skillet over medium heat, toast quinoa, stirring, until aromatic and beginning to brown. The seeds will pop about a little as they toast. Transfer quinoa to a medium saucepan. Add 2 cups water and salt. Bring to a boil over high heat and boil about 1 minute. Reduce heat to low, cover, and simmer 16 to 18 minutes or until water is absorbed. Remove lid. Stir raisins and currants into the hot quinoa. Transfer to a medium, nonreactive bowl and cool to lukewarm, about 10 minutes. Add 2 tablespoons of the oil, red pepper, snow peas, jalapeños, cumin, lemon juice, mint, cilantro, and pine nuts. Combine well. Taste and add salt, if needed. Cover and refrigerate.

4. Remove chicken from refrigerator. Pat dry with paper towels. Sprinkle with salt and pepper. In a medium, non-stick skillet, heat remaining 2 tablespoons oil over medium heat. When oil shimmers, add chicken pieces and cook, turning, until lightly browned on both sides and white throughout but still juicy, about 6 minutes. Remove chicken to a plate and cool for about 5 minutes. With fingers, tear chicken into coarse shreds. Add chicken and any accumu-lated juices to the quinoa salad, and toss to combine. Taste and adjust seasoning, if needed. Serve salad cool or at room temperature.

Serves 4

Chicken Tostada

The contrast of the crunchy crisp tortilla and raw vegetables with the tender warm chicken makes an ideal luncheon or quick supper entree. The tortillas can be fried one day in advance and stored in the cupboard in an airtight container.

1/2	cup vegetable oil
4	corn tortillas
4	fresh or frozen skinless, boneless chicken breast halves
1/2	teaspoon dried oregano, crumbled
1/2	teaspoon ground cumin
	Salt and pepper
2	cups coarsely shredded peeled carrots
1	cup shredded romaine lettuce leaves
1	cup coarsely shredded peeled jicama
1/2	red bell pepper, seeded and cut into thin strips, 2 inches by 1/8 inch
1	cup shredded Monterey Jack cheese
2	serrano chiles, minced
1/4	cup chopped fresh cilantro, loosely packed
3	tablespoons olive oil
2	tablespoons unseasoned rice vinegar
	Sour cream (optional)
	Salsa (optional)

1. In a medium skillet, heat about 1/2 cup vegetable oil over medium-high heat. When oil shimmers, fry tortillas one at a time, turning with tongs, until crisp and lightly browned on both sides, 1 to 2 minutes. Drain on paper towels. Set aside.

2. For fresh chicken, go to step 3. If breasts are frozen, place in a sealed plastic bag and thaw in a large pan of cold water for 25 to 30 minutes or until flexible. Blot with paper towels.

3. Trim fresh or thawed chicken of any visible fat. Set aside. In a small bowl, combine oregano, cumin, $1/2$ teaspoon salt and $1/8$ teaspoon pepper. Pat chicken dry and rub the seasonings over each piece. Pour all but 1 tablespoon of the oil from the skillet in which the tortillas were fried, and heat the oil left in the skillet over medium heat. Add the chicken breasts and cook, turning, until golden brown and white throughout, 8 to 10 minutes total, depending upon the thickness of the breasts. Transfer to a cutting board and let rest about 5 minutes.

4. In a large, nonreactive mixing bowl, toss together carrot, lettuce, jicama, red pepper, cheese, chiles, cilantro, olive oil, and vinegar. Season to taste with salt and pepper. To serve, place each tortilla on an individual serving plate. Pile the tossed vegetables equally among the plates, mounding a little in the centers and leaving a narrow edge of the tortilla showing. Slice each chicken breast into thin strips and arrange over the salad on each plate. Garnish with sour cream and salsa, if desired.

Serves 4

Chicken and Black-Eyed Peas Salad

Some consider it to be good luck to eat black-eyed peas for New Year's celebrations. This southern style salad fills the bill on other occasions, too. Serve it for summer picnics or informal buffets any time of the year. For safety, keep it cold until shortly before serving. Frozen or canned black-eyed peas can be used for this salad.

4   fresh or frozen skinless, boneless chicken breast halves
1   cup low-salt chicken broth, canned or homemade (page 177)
1   teaspoon dried oregano, crumbled
1   package (16 ounces) cooked frozen black-eyed peas, or 1 can (15 ounces), drained
1   medium carrot, peeled and coarsely shredded
1   medium tomato, diced
1/2 red bell pepper, seeded and chopped
1/2 green bell pepper, seeded and chopped
2   green onions, chopped
2   tablespoons chopped fresh parsley
1/2 cup bottled Italian salad dressing of choice
     Salt and freshly ground black pepper

1. For fresh chicken go to step 2. If breasts are frozen, to thaw quickly, rinse under cold running water for 3 to 5 minutes, or until flexible.

2. Trim fresh or thawed chicken of any visible fat. Cut each breast into bite-size pieces, and place in a medium saucepan with chicken broth and oregano. Bring to a boil,

then reduce heat to low. Cover and simmer until no longer pink, 4 to 5 minutes. Using a slotted spoon, transfer chicken pieces to a bowl and let cool. Save broth for some other purpose.

3. If using frozen black-eyed peas, cook according to package instructions. Drain and cool under running water. Place well-drained, cooked black-eyed peas in a large non-reactive bowl. Add all remaining ingredients and combine. Stir in the cooled chicken. Season to taste with salt and freshly ground black pepper. Cover and refrigerate for 1 to 4 hours for best texture and flavor.

Serves 4 to 6

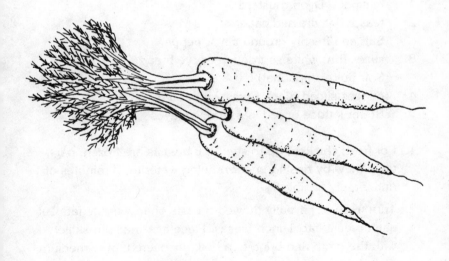

Chicken and Smoked Ham Sandwiches with Caper Mayonnaise

Accompany these classy sandwiches with champagne or sparkling wine for a real picnic or poolside delight. A selection of fresh fruit and cheese to munch on adds a nice touch.

2	fresh or frozen skinless, boneless chicken breast halves
1	cup low-salt chicken broth, canned or homemade (page 177)
1/4	cup mayonnaise, regular or lowfat
2	tablespoons chopped green bell pepper
1	teaspoon Dijon mustard
2	teaspoons drained capers
	Salt and freshly ground black pepper
8	slices firm white sourdough or rye bread
	Soft butter (optional)
4	ounces sliced Black Forest smoked ham
	Butter lettuce or red leaf lettuce leaves

1. For fresh chicken, go to step 2. If breasts are frozen, partially thaw by rinsing under running water for 3 minutes or until barely flexible.

2. Trim fresh or partially thawed breasts of any visible fat. Cut each breast into 1-inch pieces. Place in a medium skillet with the broth and bring to a boil, uncovered, over medium heat. Reduce heat to low, cover, and barely simmer until chicken is white throughout, 4 to 5 minutes. Remove

chicken pieces to a plate. When cool enough to handle, pull chicken pieces apart into coarse shreds and put in a medium, nonreactive bowl. Add mayonnaise, green pepper, mustard, and capers. Stir to combine. Season to taste with salt and pepper.

3. Butter one side of the bread slices, if desired. Divide chicken evenly among 4 bread slices. Top chicken with smoked ham slices and lettuce leaves. Cover with remaining bread slices. Cut sandwiches in half and serve.

Serves 4

Chicken, Spinach, and Walnut Salad with Chutney Dressing

A lively luncheon or light entree salad of chicken, greens, crisp bits of tart apple, and crunchy walnuts tossed with a spicy chutney dressing is loaded with flavor. Warm pumpkin or applesauce muffins taste great alongside.

Dressing:

1/4	cup vegetable oil
2	tablespoons unseasoned rice vinegar
2	tablespoons mango or peach chutney
1	teaspoon curry powder
1	teaspoon fresh lemon juice

In food processor bowl or blender jar, blend all ingredients together until smooth. Transfer to a jar or small bowl.

Salad:

2	fresh or frozen skinless, boneless chicken breast halves
2	cups low-salt chicken broth, canned or homemade (page 177), or water
1/4	cup dry white wine
	Salt
1	bunch spinach, washed, drained, dried, and torn into bite-size pieces
1	head endive, rinsed, and cut crosswise into 1/2-inch pieces
2	large firm red apples, unpeeled and cored, 1 cut into bite-size pieces, the other thinly sliced
1	rib celery, thinly sliced
1/2	cup walnut pieces

1. For fresh chicken, go to step 2. If chicken breasts are frozen, rinse under cold running water 3 to 5 minutes or until flexible.

2. Trim fresh or thawed chicken of any visible fat. Place in a medium pan with broth or water and wine. Bring to a boil over medium-high heat, then reduce heat to low, cover, and simmer until chicken is firm to the touch and white throughout, about 10 minutes. Transfer to a plate. Sprinkle lightly with salt. Cover with plastic wrap and let cool about 15 minutes. Cut breasts into thin strips and set aside.

3. In a large, nonreactive salad bowl, toss together the spinach, endive, apple pieces (reserve apple slices for garnish), celery, walnuts, and chicken. Pour salad dressing and gently toss to coat ingredients. To serve, mound salads equally in centers of four serving plates. Garnish each serving equally with apple slices.

Serves 4

Curried Chicken Salad with Melon and Grapes

This refreshing entree salad has great summertime appeal, when melons are ripe and juicy. In the fall, sliced pears can replace the melon.

4	fresh or frozen skinless, boneless chicken breast halves
	Salt
1/2	cup chopped celery
1/2	cup chopped green bell pepper
1/4	cup cashew nut pieces
2	green onions, including 2 inches of green, finely chopped
1/3	cup plain yogurt, lowfat or regular
1/3	cup mayonnaise, regular or lowfat
2	tablespoon finely chopped fresh mint
2 1/2	teaspoons Indian curry powder
1	medium cantaloupe, halved, seeded, peeled, and sliced into 1/4-inch crescents
3/4	cup *each* seedless red and green grapes
	Red curly leaf lettuce (optional)

1. For fresh chicken, go to step 2. If chicken is frozen, to thaw quickly, rinse 3 to 5 minutes under cold running water or until flexible.

2. Trim fresh or thawed breasts of any visible fat. Place in a medium skillet deep enough to hold breasts in one layer, and add cold water to cover. Bring to a boil over medium-high heat. Reduce heat and simmer until just firm to the touch and no longer pink in thickest part, 12 to 15 minutes. Remove breasts from water, place on a plate, and sprinkle

lightly with salt. Cover with plastic wrap and cool, 8 to 10 minutes.

3. When chicken is cool, cut into bite-size pieces and place in a large, nonreactive bowl. Add celery, green pepper, cashews, green onions, yogurt, mayonnaise, mint, and curry powder. Combine well to coat with dressing. Cover and refrigerate until shortly before serving.

4. To serve, mound the salad evenly in the centers of four serving plates. Arrange melon and grapes on the plates. Garnish with lettuce leaves, if desired.

Serves 4

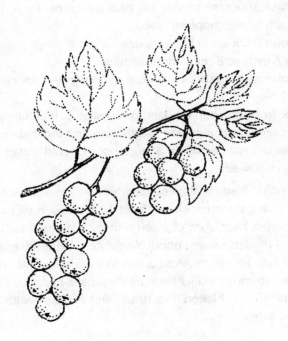

Mexican Chicken Quesadillas

Flour tortillas filled with chicken and cheese are lightly fried to crisp up the outside and melt the cheese for a tantalizing light meal. Terrific served with Mexican refried beans! Convenient frozen chicken tenders are ideal for this quick and zippy dish.

3/4   pound fresh or frozen chicken tenders (about 12 ounces)
      Salt
1   tablespoon vegetable oil, plus additional for frying
1/4   cup finely chopped onion
1/4   cup thick and chunky salsa
8   (7-inch or 8-inch) flour tortillas
4   ounces (about 1 cup) grated Monterey Jack cheese

1. For fresh chicken tenders, go to step 2. If chicken is frozen, put tenders in a sealed plastic bag and thaw about 25 minutes or until flexible in a large bowl of cold water. Blot with paper towels.

2. Sprinkle fresh or thawed chicken tenders with salt. In a medium, nonstick skillet, heat 1 tablespoon oil over medium heat. Add chicken and fry, turning 2 to 3 times, until golden brown, about 3 minutes. Using tongs, remove chicken to a plate. Add onion to the skillet and cook 2 minutes. Remove skillet from heat and stir in salsa. With fingers, shred chicken into strips, and combine with onions and salsa.

3. To assemble the quesadillas, place 4 of the tortillas on a flat surface and sprinkle each with about 2 tablespoons of the cheese. Scatter the chicken evenly among the tortillas. Sprinkle evenly with remaining cheese. Top with remaining tortillas. In a clean, medium skillet, heat about 2 teaspoons oil over medium heat. Fry quesadillas, one at a time, for 1 to 2 minutes or until lightly browned, pressing down with metal spatula. Carefully lift quesadilla with spatula, and turn. Fry second side until lightly browned, about 1 minute more. Add additional oil to the pan, as needed, for each quesadilla. Cut into quarters. Serve hot with refried beans.

Serves 4

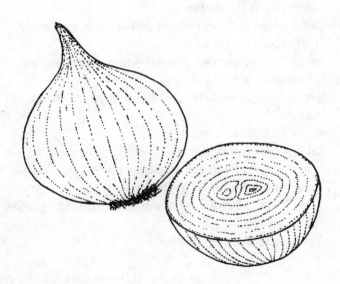

New Orleans
Hot Chicken Salad

A quick sauté of spicy chicken and colorful peppers, while still hot, are piled on chilled greens for an exceptionally exciting salad. Accompany with rustic country bread.

4	fresh or frozen skinless, boneless chicken breast halves
1	teaspoon flour
1	teaspoon paprika
1/2	teaspoon salt
1/2	teaspoon ground white pepper
1/2	teaspoon cayenne pepper
1/4	teaspoon dry mustard
3	tablespoons vegetable oil
1	large green bell pepper, seeded and cut into strips, 1 1/2 inches by 1/4 inch
1	large red bell pepper, seeded and cut into strips, 1 1/2 inches by 1/4 inch
4	green onions, including best of the green, sliced into thin rounds
2	garlic cloves, minced
1	tablespoon soft butter
1/4	cup chopped fresh dill, loosely packed
2	tablespoons chopped fresh parsley
1	head iceberg lettuce, washed, dried, torn into pieces, and refrigerated
	Vinaigrette dressing of choice

1. For fresh chicken, go to step 2. If breasts are frozen, place in a sealed plastic bag and thaw in a large pan of cold water for about 35 minutes or until flexible.

2. Trim fresh or thawed breasts of any visible fat, cut in half lengthwise, and then cut into strips 3/4 inch wide. Pat dry with paper towels. Lay chicken pieces on a platter. In a small bowl, combine flour, paprika, salt, white pepper, cayenne, and dry mustard. Season the chicken pieces with the spice mixture.

3. In a large, nonstick skillet, heat oil over medium-high heat. When oil shimmers, cook chicken, turning until no longer pink and beginning to color, 4 to 5 minutes. Using tongs, remove chicken to a bowl and keep warm. In the same skillet, cook green and red peppers, green onions, and garlic, tossing, for 1 minute. Reduce heat to low and add butter, dill, and parsley. Return chicken to the skillet. Stir to combine and heat through for 1 minute. Remove skillet from heat and keep warm while dressing lettuce.

4. In a large bowl, toss chilled lettuce with just enough vinaigrette to lightly coat. Divide lettuce among four individual serving plates. Mound warm chicken salad in centers of each plate. Serve at once.

Serves 4

Pasta and Chicken Salad

Tender bits of chicken and colorful vegetables make this pasta salad especially appealing and hearty enough for a light meal.

1	cup dry penne pasta
8	frozen chicken tenders (about 8 ounces)
	Salt
4	tablespoons olive oil
1/2	medium onion, chopped
1/2	red bell pepper, seeded and cut into thin strips, 1/8 inch by 2 inches
1	large jalapeño chile, seeded and minced
1	can (8 3/4 ounces) red kidney beans, drained and rinsed
1	can (4 ounces) sliced black olives, drained
8	cherry tomatoes, quartered
3	green onions, including 2 inches of green, chopped
1/4	cup chopped fresh cilantro, loosely packed
2	tablespoons finely chopped fresh mint
1 1/2	teaspoons ground cumin
1	tablespoon red wine vinegar
1	tablespoon unseasoned rice vinegar
	Juice of 1 lime
	Freshly ground black pepper

1. In a large pot of boiling salted water, cook pasta, uncovered, until just tender to the bite, about 12 minutes. Drain in a large colander and rinse with cold water. Shake off excess water and transfer pasta to a large, nonreactive mixing bowl. Set aside.

2. For fresh chicken, go to step 3. Place frozen chicken tenders in a sealed plastic bag and thaw in a large pan of cold water until flexible, 15 to 20 minutes. Remove to a plate and blot with paper towels.

3. Sprinkle fresh or thawed chicken tenders with salt. In a medium, nonstick skillet, heat 2 tablespoons of the oil over medium heat and cook tenders, turning, until firm to the touch and white throughout, 4 to 5 minutes. Remove to a plate and cool. In the same skillet, sauté onion, stirring, until barely softened, about 2 minutes. Scrape into bowl containing pasta. With fingers, tear cooked chicken tenders into strips. Add to pasta along with remaining ingredients and the remaining 2 tablespoons oil. Stir well to combine. Season to taste with salt and pepper.

Serves 4

Shredded Chicken Salad with Spicy Peanut Sauce

Kathy Hanley of Lake Forest, Illinois contributed this excellent entree salad recipe. The salad plates can be garnished with sliced tomatoes and cucumbers, if desired.

4	fresh or frozen skinless, boneless chicken breast halves
2	green onions, cut into 1-inch pieces
1	quarter-size slice fresh ginger, cut into slivers
1	tablespoon dry sherry
1/4	teaspoon salt
1/4	teaspoon plus 2 tablespoons sugar
1 1/2	tablespoons creamy peanut butter
2 1/2	tablespoons vegetable oil
2	tablespoons soy sauce
1 1/2	tablespoons unseasoned rice vinegar
1/2	teaspoon sesame oil
1/4	teaspoon cayenne
2	tablespoons chopped fresh cilantro
1/2	tablespoon minced white onion
6	cups shredded iceberg lettuce

1. For fresh chicken breasts, go to step 2. If breasts are frozen, place in sealed plastic bag and thaw in a large pan of cold water until barely flexible, 25 to 30 minutes.

2. Place fresh or partially thawed breasts in a 2-quart pan and pour in 3 cups of water. Add green onions, ginger, sherry, salt, and 1/4 teaspoon sugar. Bring to a boil over medium-high heat, then reduce heat to low, cover, and simmer for 20 to 25 minutes or until chicken is white throughout the

thickest part. Remove to a plate, cover with plastic wrap, and let stand until cool enough to handle. With fingers, pull chicken apart into long shreds. Place in a medium bowl, cover, and refrigerate until ready to use, up to one day ahead.

3. In a medium bowl or blender jar, mix well the peanut butter, oil, soy sauce, 2 tablespoons sugar, rice vinegar, sesame oil, and cayenne. Stir in cilantro and onion. Mound 1 1/2 cups of lettuce on each of four serving plates. Arrange chicken equally over the lettuce. Drizzle peanut sauce equally over all. Serve cold.

Serves 4

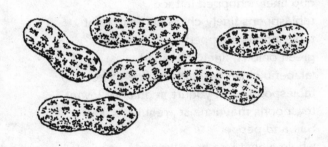

Spicy Chicken
Whole-Wheat Pitas

Whole-wheat pita bread rounds filled with spicy broiled chicken tenders and a refreshing mint and cilantro-flavored garnish make sandwiches to rave about.

12	fresh or frozen chicken tenders (about 12 ounces)
1 1/2	teaspoons chile powder
1	teaspoon ground cumin
1/2	teaspoon dried oregano, crumbled
1/2	teaspoon salt
1	large garlic clove, pressed
2	teaspoons fresh lemon juice
1	teaspoon olive oil
1	cup finely chopped lettuce
3	tablespoons finely chopped fresh mint
2	tablespoons chopped fresh cilantro
2	green onions, finely chopped
1	jalapeño chile, seeded and finely chopped
1	tablespoon plain yogurt, regular or lowfat
2	teaspoons mayonnaise, regular or lowfat
	Salt and pepper
4	whole-wheat pita bread rounds, or whole-wheat tortillas
	Sliced tomatoes and cucumbers

1. For fresh chicken tenders, go to step 2. If tenders are frozen, rinse under cold running water about 3 minutes or until flexible. Blot with paper towels.

2. Cut each fresh or thawed tender in half lengthwise. Place in a medium, nonreactive bowl. Add chile powder, cumin,

oregano, salt, garlic, lemon juice, and oil. Toss to coat with seasonings. Let sit 20 minutes.

3. Meanwhile, in a medium bowl, combine lettuce, mint, cilantro, green onions, jalapeño, yogurt, and mayonnaise. Season to taste with salt and pepper. Set aside.

4. Preheat oven broiler and place rack in top position. Arrange chicken tenders on a foil-lined baking sheet and broil 4 to 5 minutes or until sizzling and cooked throughout.

5. To serve, cut top third from each pita round. Fill equally with tenders and lettuce mixture. Garnish with tomatoes and cucumbers.

Serves 4

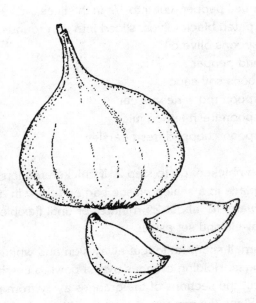

California Chicken, Fennel, and Orange Salad

Sweet juicy oranges and crisp raw fennel are a delicious combination. Add sautéed chicken tenders and California black olives for a light entree salad.

8	fresh or frozen chicken tenders (about 1/2 pound)
2	large navel oranges
1	medium fennel bulb, trimmed, halved, and thinly sliced crosswise
1	cup finely shredded red cabbage
4	large romaine lettuce leaves, washed, dried, and torn into bite-size pieces
1/2	green bell pepper, cut into 1/8-inch slices
10	large pitted black olives, sliced into thin rounds
4	tablespoons olive oil
	Salt and pepper
2	teaspoons soy sauce
1	tablespoon red wine vinegar
1	tablespoon fresh lemon juice
1	tablespoon chopped fresh parsley

1. For fresh chicken, go to step 2. If chicken tenders are frozen, place in a sealed plastic bag and thaw in a large pan of cold water for about 25 minutes or until flexible. Blot with paper towels and set aside.

2. With a small sharp knife, cut away skin and white pith from the oranges. Holding oranges over a bowl to catch the juices, cut the sections of the oranges away from the membranes. Place the separated orange sections in a large, non-

reactive salad bowl. Add fennel, cabbage, romaine, green pepper, and olives. Cover and refrigerate.

3. In a large skillet, heat 2 tablespoons of the oil over medium heat. Add fresh or thawed chicken tenders. Season lightly with salt and pepper. Cook 2 to 3 minutes, turn over, and sprinkle with the soy sauce. Cook second side 2 to 3 minutes or until white throughout but still juicy. Transfer chicken and juices from the skillet to a plate and cool for about 10 minutes. Meanwhile, toss the salad with remaining 2 tablespoons oil, vinegar, lemon juice, and parsley. Taste and season with salt and freshly ground black pepper. Using tongs, mound salad loosely on four serving plates. Cut cooled chicken tenders in half lengthwise. Arrange evenly on top of the salads. Serve at once.

Serves 4

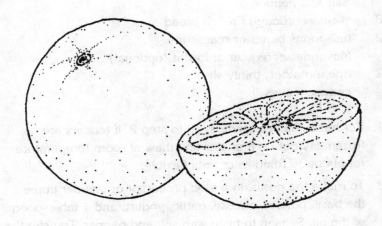

Chicken Sandwiches with Pesto and Tomato

Sandwiches make a quick and satisfying meal, and they can be more healthful, too, if you go light on fatty spreads. Convenient and juicy chicken tenders have become widely available in many supermarkets, either fresh or individually frozen in economy-sized packages.

12	fresh or frozen chicken tenders (about 12 ounces)
1	cup fresh basil leaves, lightly packed
1/4	cup chopped fresh parsley
2	tablespoons freshly ground Parmesan cheese
1	garlic clove, chopped
2	tablespoons plain yogurt, regular or lowfat
2	tablespoons olive oil
	Salt and pepper
8	slices sourdough French bread
2	teaspoons butter or margarine
	Mayonnaise, regular or lowfat (optional)
2	ripe tomatoes, thinly sliced
	Lettuce leaves

1. For fresh chicken tenders, go to step 2. If tenders are frozen, lay out on a platter and thaw at room temperature for about 30 minutes or until flexible.

2. To make the pesto, in a food processor or blender puree the basil, parsley, cheese, garlic, yogurt, and 1 tablespoon of the oil. Season to taste with salt and pepper. Transfer the pesto to a bowl and set aside.

3. Cut fresh or thawed tenders in half lengthwise. Pat dry with paper towels. Sprinkle with salt and pepper. Heat remaining 1 tablespoon of the oil in a large, nonstick skillet over medium heat. Add the chicken strips and cook, turning frequently, until golden brown and white throughout, 4 to 5 minutes. Remove to a plate.

4. Preheat oven broiler. Spread one side of the bread with about 1/2 teaspoon butter. Toast lightly, under broiler, on both sides. Spread the buttered sides with mayonnaise, if desired. Layer with chicken strips, pesto, tomato slices, lettuce, and more pesto. Top with remaining bread. Cut each sandwich in half and serve.

Serves 4

Chicken Sandwiches with Red Onion Marmalade

Slightly sweet and a little tart, onion marmalade is made by cooking onions slowly until they're soft and flavorful. Pile some over chicken on French rolls for super sandwiches. They'll score raves at a football party.

4	tablespoons olive oil plus additional for rolls
2	medium red onions, coarsely chopped
2	large shallots, chopped
1/4	cup sugar
2	tablespoons red wine vinegar
	Salt and freshly ground pepper
4	fresh or frozen skinless, boneless chicken breast halves
4	(6-inch) French rolls, halved lengthwise
	Lettuce
	Mayonnaise, regular or lowfat, and mustard (optional)

1. In a heavy, medium skillet, heat 2 tablespoons oil over medium heat. Add onions and shallots. Stir well. Reduce heat to low, cover, and cook until very soft but not brown, stirring occasionally, for about 35 minutes. Add sugar and vinegar. Cook uncovered over medium-low heat until most of the liquid evaporates, stirring frequently, for about 10 minutes. Season to taste with salt and plenty of pepper. Serve the marmalade warm, or cover and refrigerate up to 3 days. (If refrigerated, bring to room temperature before serving.)

2. For fresh chicken, go to step 3. If chicken breasts are frozen, to thaw quickly, rinse under cold running water for 3 to 5 minutes or until flexible. Blot with paper towels.

3. Trim fresh or thawed breasts of any visible fat. Place breasts between two sheets of plastic wrap and pound with the flat side of a meat mallet or a rolling pin to an even thickness of 1/4 inch. Sprinkle lightly with salt and pepper. In a large, nonstick skillet, heat remaining 2 tablespoons oil over medium heat. Cook chicken without crowding, turning, until lightly browned on both sides and white throughout but still juicy, 6 to 8 minutes total.

4. Preheat oven broiler. Brush cut sides of rolls with olive oil. Broil with the cut sides toward heat until golden brown. Spread bottom half of each roll with about one-quarter of the warm onion marmalade. Top each with a warm chicken breast and lettuce. Spread top half of each roll with mayonnaise and/or mustard, if desired. Close sandwiches and cut in half.

Serves 4

2

Top-o'-the Stove or Outdoor Grill

Stove-top cooking and outdoor grilling are generally quick, easy, and fun to do. Boneless, skinless chicken breast halves are perfect for this method of cooking, and nearly every recipe in this chapter uses them. Fresh chicken breasts can go from market to stove right away, or you can simply pull a few frozen breasts from the freezer and thaw them while preparing the other ingredients needed for the chosen recipe. A wonderful main course can be ready to serve in about one hour.

When sautéeing, frying, or grilling the breasts, it's easy to watch what's happening in the pan and control the process, to avoid over- or undercooking the delicate meat. When chicken breasts are gently poached in a liquid, such as water, stock, or wine, they become moist and tender. Adding herbs, spices, and a few chopped vegetables infuses subtle flavors to the chicken, and the resulting broth is delicious and useful for sauces and soups. When braising breasts, they are first browned in oil or butter, then vegetables and all sorts of seasonings are added along with a small amount of wine, broth, or perhaps tomatoes. Gentle simmering finishes the dish as it creates its own flavorful sauce.

Outdoor grilling, too, is quick and easy, with the bonus of not heating up the kitchen during hot weather. Casual outdoor entertaining continues to be very popular and calls for firing up the barbecue. With improved equipment, outdoor cooking is possible in many parts of the country throughout most of the year. In this chapter, you'll find grilling recipes that are surefire winners. Family members and guests alike will be ready, fork in hand, to dig in when the cook announces, "Come and get it while it's hot!"

Watching over the pans on the stove and tending the barbecue grill are creative ways to cook. This chapter offers many delicious ways to enjoy the process.

Brandied Chicken

Brandy gives this simple dish a distinctive flavor. This dish can be prepared in a hurry, even with frozen chicken. Serve with oven-roasted potatoes or baked butternut squash.

4	fresh or frozen skinless, boneless chicken breast halves
	Salt and pepper
2	tablespoons olive oil
2	medium tomatoes, peeled and chopped, or 1 cup canned chopped tomatoes
1/3	cup dry white wine
2	tablespoons brandy or cognac
2	garlic cloves, pressed
1	tablespoon chopped fresh Italian flat-leaf parsley

1. For fresh chicken, go to step 2. If chicken breasts are frozen, to thaw quickly, rinse under cold running water for 3 to 5 minutes or until flexible. Blot with paper towels.

2. Trim fresh or thawed breasts of any visible fat. Sprinkle lightly with salt and pepper. In a large, nonstick skillet, heat oil over medium heat and brown the chicken, turning 2 to 3 times, for about 5 minutes. Remove breasts to a plate. Add the tomatoes, wine, brandy, garlic, and parsley. Return chicken to the pan. Cover, reduce heat to low, and simmer for about 10 to 12 minutes or until chicken is white throughout. Transfer to a serving dish and serve.

Serves 4

Grilled Garlic-Lemon Chicken

Chicken on the grill flavored with garlic and lemon is always welcome, and it goes well with all your favorite picnic and outdoor foods.

4	fresh or frozen skinless, boneless chicken breast halves
2	large garlic cloves, pressed
1/4	teaspoon salt
1/8	teaspoon pepper
2	tablespoons fresh lemon juice
2	tablespoons olive oil

1. For fresh chicken, go to step 2. If breasts are frozen, to thaw quickly, rinse under cold running water about 3 to 5 minutes or until flexible. Blot with paper towels.

2. Trim fresh or thawed breasts of any visible fat, and place in a medium, nonreactive bowl. Add garlic, salt, pepper, lemon juice, and olive oil. Turn chicken several times to coat with marinade. Cover and marinate 1 to 2 hours in the refrigerator.

3. Prepare a hot fire in a barbecue grill. Oil the grill. When coals are ready, remove breasts from the marinade, shaking off excess, and place on hot grill. Cook until lightly browned, about 6 minutes. Turn and brush with marinade. Grill second side 4 to 6 minutes or until white throughout but still juicy.

Serves 4

Chicken with Three Salsas

Chicken with salsa has become a favorite combination just about everywhere. The sale of commercial salsas has surpassed the sale of catsup, and the great variety of salsas now available surely points to its popularity. Fresh salsa is easy to make and tastes absolutely delicious when eaten with grilled, broiled, or sautéed chicken breast, so this recipe offers three different fresh salsas. Enjoy the lively flavor of salsa one at a time, or if you're throwing a party, make all three to accompany a platter of juicy chicken breasts. Steamed rice or a simple pilaf are perfect additions to the menu.

Salsa Fresca Mexicana:
This fresh Mexican salsa is often just called "salsa."

3	medium ripe tomatoes, finely chopped
1/3	cup finely chopped white onion
2	to 3 serrano chiles, minced (seeded, if desired)
1	small garlic clove, minced
1/4	cup chopped fresh cilantro
3	tablespoons fresh lime juice
	Salt to taste

In a medium, nonreactive bowl, stir all ingredients together. Serve within 1 to 4 hours for freshest flavor and texture.

(recipe continues)

Fresh Corn Salsa:
Frozen corn works, but fresh is definitely best!

2   large ears fresh corn, shucked, or 1 1/2 cups frozen corn
1   medium tomato, seeded and finely chopped
1/4   medium white onion, minced
1/4   medium red bell pepper, seeded and finely diced
1   to 2 serrano or jalapeño chiles, seeded and minced
2   tablespoons fresh lime juice
1/2   teaspoon ground cumin
2   tablespoons chopped fresh cilantro
      Salt and freshly ground black pepper

In a large pan of boiling water, cook ears of corn or frozen corn until barely tender, 2 to 3 minutes. Drain and rinse under cold running water. Cut kernels off cobs and place in a medium, nonreactive bowl. Add remaining ingredients and stir to combine. Serve at room temperature. Best if used within 6 hours.

Fresh Mango Salsa:
Tropical fruits make fabulous salsas.

1   large ripe mango, peeled and finely diced
1/4   medium white onion, finely chopped
1/4   medium red bell pepper, seeded and finely diced
1   large jalapeño chile, seeded and finely chopped
2   tablespoons fresh lime juice
1   tablespoon finely chopped fresh mint leaves
      Salt to taste

In a medium, nonreactive bowl, stir all ingredients together. Cover and let stand about 30 minutes, or refrigerate up to 6 hours for freshest flavor and texture.

Chicken:

The breasts can be sautéed, grilled, or oven-broiled. This recipe sautées.

4   fresh or frozen skinless, boneless chicken breast halves
1   garlic clove, crushed
     Salt and pepper
2   tablespoons olive oil

1. For fresh chicken, go to step 2. If breasts are frozen, place in a large sealed plastic bag and thaw in a large pan of cold water for about 35 minutes or until flexible.

2. Trim fresh or thawed breasts of any visible fat. Pat dry with paper towels. Rub the garlic over the breasts and season with salt and pepper. In a large, nonstick skillet, heat oil over medium heat. When oil shimmers, add chicken and cook, turning, until lightly browned on both sides and white throughout, 8 to 10 minutes total. Serve breasts hot with salsa of choice.

Serves 4

Aegean Chicken with Fennel and Tomatoes

Chicken and vegetables with an Aegean flair. Serve with penne or orzo pasta.

4	fresh or frozen skinless, boneless chicken breast halves
2	tablespoons flour
	Salt and pepper
3	tablespoons olive oil
6	ripe roma tomatoes, peeled and chopped, or 1 1/2 cups canned crushed tomatoes
1	medium onion, chopped
1	medium fennel bulb, trimmed, halved lengthwise, and sliced crosswise
1/2	green bell pepper, seeded and cut into 1/4-inch dices
3	garlic cloves, chopped
1	teaspoon dried oregano, crumbled
1/2	teaspoon crushed red pepper flakes
1/4	teaspoon ground allspice
2	tablespoons fresh lemon juice

1. For fresh chicken, go to step 2. If breasts are frozen, place in a sealed plastic bag and thaw in a large pan of cold water for 25 to 30 minutes or until flexible. Blot with paper towels.

2. Trim fresh or thawed breasts of any visible fat and cut into 1-inch pieces. Pat chicken dry with paper towels. Dust chicken pieces lightly with flour, and sprinkle with salt and pepper. In a large, nonstick skillet, heat 2 tablespoons of the olive oil over medium heat. When oil shimmers, add

chicken pieces and cook, stirring, until light brown on the outside and white throughout, about 3 to 4 minutes. With a slotted spoon, remove chicken pieces to a bowl. In the same skillet, heat remaining tablespoon of oil. Add tomatoes, onion, fennel, green pepper, garlic, oregano, red pepper flakes, and allspice. Stir to combine, then cover and cook, stirring occasionally, until vegetables are tender, 8 to 10 minutes. Return chicken pieces and any accumulated juices to the pan. Stir in lemon juice. Season to taste with salt and pepper. Serve.

Serves 4

Breast of Chicken with Basil Cream and Pine Nuts

Fresh basil in a light cream sauce and toasted pine nuts make an elegant topping for boneless chicken breasts. Polenta or garlic mashed potatoes are excellent alongside.

1/4	cup pine nuts
4	fresh or frozen skinless, boneless chicken breast halves
1/2	teaspoon salt
1/8	teaspoon pepper
2	tablespoons olive oil
2	teaspoons flour
2	tablespoons dry vermouth or dry white wine
1	cup low-salt chicken broth, canned or homemade (page 177)
1/8	teaspoon crushed red pepper flakes
1/4	cup whipping cream
1/2	cup finely shredded fresh basil, loosely packed

1. In a small, dry, heavy skillet, toast pine nuts over medium heat, tossing frequently, for about 2 minutes or until they turn a golden brown. (Watch them carefully. They can burn quickly and become bitter.) Reserve in a small bowl.

2. For fresh chicken, go to step 3. If chicken breasts are frozen, to thaw quickly, rinse under cold running water 3 to 5 minutes or until flexible. Blot with paper towels.

3. Trim fresh or thawed breasts of any visible fat. Place each breast between two sheets of plastic wrap and pound with flat side of a meat mallet or a rolling pin to an even thickness of about $1/3$ inch. Season with salt and pepper. In a large, nonstick skillet, heat oil over medium heat. Add chicken and cook 3 to 4 minutes until lightly browned. Turn and cook 2 to 3 minutes longer or until white throughout. Transfer to a plate and keep warm in a 200° oven.

4. Stir flour into the pan drippings. Add vermouth and chicken broth. Bring to a boil, stirring, and cook about 2 minutes. Stir in red pepper flakes and cream. Reduce heat to medium-low and simmer until thickened, 2 to 3 minutes. Taste and adjust seasoning if needed. Stir in basil shreds. Turn off heat. Remove chicken from oven and arrange on a serving platter or on individual plates. Pour accumulated juices into the skillet and combine with the sauce. Spoon evenly over chicken. Garnish each serving equally with the reserved toasted pine nuts. Serve hot.

Serves 4

Chicken with Cherries

This is a revised and updated version of the chicken and cherries combination. It's less rich, but no less delicious. To add a bright spark of color to the plate, serve spears of broccoli alongside.

4	fresh or frozen skinless, boneless chicken breast halves
1	can (16 1/2 ounces) black Bing cherries
1/2	cup low-salt chicken broth,canned or homemade (page 177)
2	tablespoons dry sherry
1/8	teaspoon ground allspice
1/8	teaspoon cinnamon
1/8	teaspoon ground ginger
1	tablespoon balsamic vinegar
1	tablespoon cornstarch
2	tablespoons flour
1/2	teaspoon salt
1/4	teaspoon pepper
1/4	teaspoon paprika
1	tablespoon unsalted butter
1	tablespoon vegetable oil
	Parsley sprigs (optional)

1. For fresh chicken, go to step 2. If chicken breasts are frozen, place in sealed plastic bag and thaw in a large pan of cold water for 25 to 30 minues or until flexible. Blot with paper towels.

2. Trim fresh or thawed breasts of any visible fat. Place breasts between two sheets of plastic wrap and pound with

flat side of a meat mallet or a rolling pin to an even thickness of about 1/4 inch. Set aside.

3. To make the sauce, strain the juice from the cherries into a medium saucepan. Reserve the cherries in a bowl. To the saucepan, add broth, sherry, allspice, cinnamon, ginger, balsamic vinegar, and cornstarch. Bring to a boil over medium heat and cook, stirring, until thickened and clear, 1 to 2 minutes. Stir in the cherries and set aside.

4. In a pie plate, combine flour, salt, pepper, and paprika. Pat chicken dry with paper towels. Dredge breasts with flour mixture. Shake off excess. In a heavy, large skillet, heat butter and oil over medium heat. When butter foams, add chicken and sauté, turning, until golden brown on both sides, 4 to 6 minutes total. Reheat cherry sauce.

5. To serve, pour about 1/4 cup cherry sauce on each of four serving plates. Top each serving with one chicken breast, and arrange a few cherries on each plate. Garnish one side of each plate with a sprig of parsley, if desired.

Serves 4

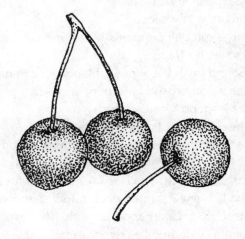

Chinese Chicken Stir-Fry on Pan-Fried Noodle Cakes

Individual pan-fried noodle cakes with a chicken and vegetable topping is a terrific and imaginative entree. You'll need one or two (6-inch) nonstick skillets to fry the noodle cakes. A wok or regular skillet can be used for the chicken and vegetables.

	Vegetable oil for frying
1	pound fresh or dried Chinese egg noodles
3	tablespoons soy sauce
8	fresh or frozen chicken tenders (about 8 ounces)
1	tablespoon oyster sauce
1	teaspoon cornstarch
2	teaspoons dry sherry
1	teaspoon minced fresh ginger
1	garlic clove, minced
1/4	teaspoon sesame oil
1/2	onion, thinly sliced
1/2	large red bell pepper, seeded and cut into strips 1 1/2 inches by 1/4 inch
1/4	pound fresh snow peas, blanched 1 minute
1/4	teaspoon crushed red pepper flakes
1	tablespoon Chinese plum sauce
2	green onions, finely chopped
2	tablespoons toasted white sesame seeds

1. Brush 4 (6-inch) shallow soup plates with oil. In a large pot of boiling salted water, cook noodles according to package instructions. Drain and toss with 1 tablespoon of the soy sauce. Divide noodles evenly among the soup plates,

pressing to form into round cakes. Cover each bowl with plastic wrap, pressing it directly on the noodles, and refrigerate until ready to use.

2. For fresh chicken, go to step 3. If chicken tenders are frozen, place in a sealed plastic bag and thaw in a large pan of cold water until flexible, about 25 minutes.

3. Cut fresh or thawed chicken tenders into $1/2$-inch strips and set aside. In a medium bowl, combine the remaining 2 tablespoons of soy sauce, oyster sauce, cornstarch, sherry, ginger, garlic, and sesame oil. Add chicken strips. Stir to coat chicken with marinade, then cover the bowl and refrigerate 1 to 6 hours.

4. Shortly before serving, heat 2 teaspoons oil over medium-high heat in each of two small (6-inch), nonstick skillets. Slide noodle cakes into each skillet. Cook until golden brown on the bottom, 4 to 6 minutes. Invert cakes onto a plate, one at a time, and slide back into the skillet, adding more oil if needed to prevent sticking. Cook second side until brown, 4 to 6 minutes. Transfer to oiled cookie sheet. Keep warm in 200° oven. Repeat with two remaining noodle cakes.

5. In a wok or medium, nonstick skillet, heat 1 tablespoon oil over medium-high heat. Add onion, red pepper, snow peas, and crushed red pepper. Cook, tossing, for 2 minutes. With slotted spoon, remove vegetables to a bowl. Add chicken strips and the marinade. Cook, stirring, until chicken looks white on the surface, 2 to 3 minutes. Return vegetables to the wok or skillet. Stir in plum sauce and green onions. Cook, stirring, until bubbling. Place each noodle cake on a serving plate. Divide chicken topping evenly over each cake. Sprinkle with toasted sesame seeds. Serve at once.

Serves 4

Grilled Chicken Breasts with Chipotle Vinaigrette

Here's a real treat for those who like it hot. The easy and fiery vinaigrette is seasoned with chipotle chiles, which are dried, smoked jalapeños. They can be found, canned, in Latin American food stores, specialty food shops, and many supermarkets.

1/4	cup fresh orange juice
2 1/2	tablespoons unseasoned rice vinegar
2	tablespoons fresh lime juice
1	tablespoon chopped fresh cilantro
1/2	teaspoon Worcestershire sauce
2	canned chipotle chiles, seeded and mashed
1	teaspoon sugar
1	tablespoon olive oil
	Salt
4	fresh or frozen skinless, boneless chicken breast halves
	Vegetable oil
	Pepper

1. In a small bowl, combine orange juice, vinegar, lime juice, cilantro, Worcestershire sauce, chipotles, and sugar. Gradually whisk in the olive oil, or puree vinaigrette in blender jar. Season to taste with salt. Can be made 1 day ahead. Cover and refrigerate until shortly before serving.

2. For fresh chicken breasts, go to step 3. If breasts are frozen, rinse under cold running water 3 to 5 minutes or until flexible. Blot with paper towels.

3. Prepare a hot fire in a barbecue grill. Trim fresh or thawed breasts of any visible fat. Brush with vegetable oil and sprinkle with salt and pepper. When coals are hot, place breasts on oiled grill rack, and grill 4 to 6 minutes on each side or until lightly browned and white throughout. Remove to a platter or individual serving plates. Spoon a little vinaigrette over the chicken and serve. Pass remaining vinaigrette at the table.

Serves 4

Chicken Esterhazy

Inspired by a classic dish, which carries the name of a former Hungarian royal family, I have substituted chicken for the usual beef, with excellent results. This unique and stylish dish has great color and flavor. It's just right for a special occasion.

4	fresh or frozen skinless, boneless chicken breast halves
1	tablespoon unsalted butter
3	tablespoons vegetable oil
1/2	medium onion, finely chopped
2	shallots, finely chopped
1	medium carrot, finely chopped
2	tablespoons flour
2	cups low-salt chicken broth, canned or homemade (page 177)
1/4	cup dry white wine
1	tablespoon fresh lemon juice
2	bay leaves
3	whole allspice or 1/8 teaspoon ground allspice
1/4	teaspoon dried thyme leaves
	Pinch crushed red pepper flakes
2	tablespoons chopped smoked ham (lean part of smoked ham hock is good)
1/2	cup heavy cream
	Salt
1	medium parsnip, peeled and cut into slivers 2 inches long
1	medium carrot, peeled and cut into slivers 2 inches long
1/2	red bell pepper, seeded and cut into slivers 2 inches long
2	baby dill pickles, cut into lengthwise slivers
	Chopped fresh parsley

1. For fresh chicken breasts, go to step 2. If chicken breasts are frozen, place in a sealed plastic bag and thaw in a large

pan of cold water until flexible, 25 to 30 minutes. Blot with paper towels.

2. Trim fresh or thawed breasts of any visible fat. Place breasts between two pieces of plastic wrap and pound with flat side of a meat mallet or a rolling pin to an even thickness of $1/2$ inch. Set aside while making the sauce.

3. In a heavy, medium saucepan, heat butter and 1 tablespoon of the oil over medium heat. Add onion, shallots, and carrot. Cook, stirring frequently, until golden. Stir in flour and cook 30 seconds. Remove pan from heat and add chicken broth, wine, and lemon juice all at once. Whisk to combine. Return pan to medium-high heat and cook, whisking, until sauce thickens. Add bay, allspice, thyme, pepper flakes, and ham. Reduce heat to medium and cook until sauce is reduced by one-third, about 15 minutes. Strain sauce through a wire sieve into a medium bowl. Discard the solids. Return sauce to a clean pan. Stir in the cream and bring sauce to a boil. Reduce heat to low and cook, stirring frequently, until sauce is smooth and thickened, about 5 minutes. Taste and season with salt, if needed. Cover and set aside.

4. In a small pan of boiling water, cook parsnip, carrot, and red pepper separately, until barely tender, 1 to 3 minutes. Drain and transfer to a bowl. Salt lightly. Cover and set aside.

5. Sprinkle chicken breasts lightly with salt. In a large skillet, heat remaining 2 tablespoons oil over medium-high heat and cook chicken until lightly browned on both sides and white throughout, 6 to 8 minutes total. Reheat the sauce and vegetables. Arrange chicken breasts on a warmed platter or individual plates. Spoon warmed sauce over the breasts, letting some sauce pool onto the plates. Scatter the vegetables and pickles on top. Sprinkle with parsley and serve at once.

Serves 4

Chicken with German Onion Sauce

This aromatic mild onion sauce is especially good with buttered egg noodles. The sauce can be made up to three days ahead, then covered and refrigerated. Reheat the sauce while the chicken cooks.

4	tablespoons unsalted butter
1	large onion, minced
3	tablespoons flour
2	cups canned beef broth
1	tablespoon dry white wine
	Salt and freshly ground black pepper
6	fresh or frozen skinless, boneless chicken breast halves
3	tablespoons vegetable oil
2	tablespoons finely chopped fresh parsley

1. In a heavy, medium saucepan, melt butter over medium heat. Add onion and cook, stirring, until onion is soft and golden brown, 5 to 6 minutes. Adjust heat, as necessary, to avoid too much browning. Add flour, and cook 1 minute. Remove pan from heat and whisk in broth and wine all at once. When combined, return pan to heat, bring to a boil, and cook, stirring, until thickened. Reduce heat to low, cover, and simmer 5 minutes, stirring frequently. Season to taste with salt and pepper. Reserve off heat, or cover and refrigerate up to 3 days. Reheat shortly before serving.

2. For fresh chicken, go to step 3. If chicken breasts are frozen, to thaw quickly, rinse under cold running water 3 to 5 minutes or until flexible. Blot with paper towels.

3. Trim fresh or thawed breasts of any visible fat. Season lightly with salt and pepper. In a heavy, large skillet, heat oil over medium heat. Sauté chicken about 4 to 5 minutes on each side or until lightly browned and white throughout but still juicy. Serve at once with heated onion sauce spooned over. Sprinkle with parsley. Pass extra sauce at the table.

Serves 6

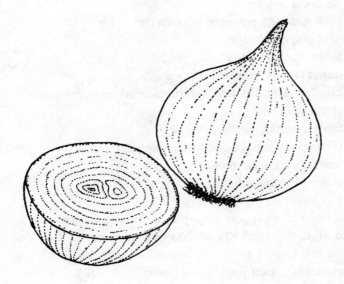

Chicken Breasts with Ginger-Orange Sauce

Fresh ginger and orange zest impart a lively flavored punch to the speedy skillet sauce for this elegant chicken dish.

4	fresh or frozen skinless, boneless chicken breast halves
	Salt and pepper
2	tablespoons vegetable or olive oil
2	shallots, minced
1	tablespoon minced fresh ginger
2	garlic cloves, pressed
1/2	cup low-salt chicken broth, canned or homemade (page 177)
2	tablespoons dry sherry
1/2	tablespoon unseasoned rice vinegar
1/2	teaspoon orange zest
1/2	cup heavy cream

1. For fresh chicken, go to step 2. If chicken breasts are frozen, to thaw quickly, place in a sealed plastic bag and thaw in a large pan of cold water for 25 to 30 minutes or until flexible. Blot with paper towels.

2. Trim fresh or thawed breasts of any visible fat. Place breasts between two sheets of plastic wrap and pound to an even thickness of 1/3 inch. Sprinkle lightly with salt and pepper. In a large, nonstick skillet, heat oil over medium heat. Add chicken breasts and cook, turning until lightly browned and white throughout but still juicy, 6 to 8 minutes total. Remove breasts to a plate and keep warm.

3. To the skillet, add shallots, ginger, and garlic. Cook, stirring rapidly, 1 minute. Add chicken broth, sherry, rice vinegar, and orange zest. Bring to a boil and cook 2 to 3 minutes until reduced by about one-third. Add cream and cook until slightly thickened, about 3 minutes. Season to taste with salt and pepper. Serve over the chicken breasts.

Serves 4

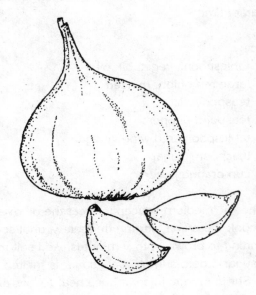

Grilled Chicken Breasts with Red Onion Sauce and Summer Squash Medley

Fire up the barbecue for a healthy plate of grilled chicken and a colorful medley of grilled summer squash. To allow undivided attention at the grill, make the tangy red onion sauce ahead of time.

Sauce:

2	tablespoons vegetable oil
1	large red onion, minced
1	teaspoon salt
1/8	teaspoon pepper
1 1/2	tablespoons red wine vinegar
1 1/2	teaspoons sugar
1/2	cup orange juice

In a heavy, medium saucepan, heat the oil over medium heat and cook the onion, stirring frequently, until softened and just beginning to brown, 4 to 5 minutes. Add salt, pepper, vinegar, and sugar. Cook, stirring, until sugar is melted, about 2 minutes. Stir in orange juice, reduce heat to low, and simmer until thickened, about 5 minutes. Transfer to a bowl, cover, and refrigerate for up to 2 days. Reheat shortly before using.

Chicken and Squash:

4   fresh or frozen skinless, boneless chicken breast halves
2   garlic cloves, minced
1 1/2   tablespoons olive oil plus additional for grilling
1   teaspoon salt
1/4   teaspoon pepper
4   small yellow crookneck squash, rinsed and cut in half lengthwise
4   small pattypan summer squash, rinsed and cut in half crosswise
2   medium zucchini, cut on a diagonal into elongated ovals, about 1/3-inch thick

1. Prepare a hot fire in a barbecue grill. Oil the grill. For fresh chicken breasts, go to step 2. If breasts are frozen, to thaw quickly, rinse under cold running water for 3 to 5 minutes or until flexible.

2. Trim fresh or thawed breasts of any visible fat. Pat dry with paper towels. Place on a plate. In a small bowl, combine garlic, olive oil, salt, and pepper. Rub half the garlic mixture over the chicken breasts. Place all the squash pieces on a separate large plate, and rub the other half of the garlic mixture over the squash pieces.

3. When the coals are ready, oil the grill again to prevent sticking, and lay squash pieces, cut side down, around the outside edge of the grill. Lay chicken breasts in center of grill, over the hottest coals. Using tongs, turn squash frequently, brushing with additional oil, if needed, and grill until tender, 8 to 10 minutes. Grill chicken 4 to 5 minutes on each side or until white throughout but still juicy. To serve, arrange the vegetables and chicken breasts on a large warmed platter. Reheat the onion sauce and place in a small serving bowl.

Serves 4

Herbed Chicken with Bow-Tie Pasta

The delightful shape of bow-tie pasta, known as farfalle, has great eye-appeal. This recipe uses yogurt for its lowfat creamy sauce, making this dish even more appealing. Fresh basil is very important for the flavor and appearance of this dish.

4   fresh or frozen skinless, boneless chicken breast halves
     Salt and freshly ground black pepper
1   cup plain yogurt, lowfat or regular
1 1/2 teaspoons cornstarch
3/4   cup chopped fresh basil, loosely packed
1/2   teaspoon dried oregano, crumbled
1/8   teaspoon crushed red pepper flakes
1   pound dry farfalle (bow-tie) pasta
2   tablespoons olive oil
1   medium red bell pepper, seeded and cut into strips, about
     2 inches by 1/4 inch
1/2   cup chopped onion
2   large garlic cloves, chopped
1/2   cup low-salt chicken broth, canned or homemade
     (page 177)
     Fresh basil sprigs

1. For fresh chicken, go to step 2. If breasts are frozen, to thaw quickly, rinse under cold running water for 3 to 5 minutes or until flexible.

2. Trim fresh or thawed breasts of any visible fat and cut into strips 1/2 inch wide. Blot with paper towels. Place on a plate, sprinkle with salt and pepper, and set aside.

3. In a small bowl, mix yogurt, cornstarch, basil, oregano, and pepper flakes. Set aside.

4. Bring a large pot of salted water to a boil, and cook pasta according to package directions. (Pasta usually requires 12 to 15 minutes to cook.)

5. Meanwhile, in a large, nonstick skillet, heat oil over medium heat. Add chicken and cook, turning, until no longer pink, 4 to 5 minutes. With slotted spoon, remove chicken to a plate. To the same skillet, add red pepper, onion, and garlic. Cook, stirring, until vegetables soften, 3 to 4 minutes. Stir in yogurt mixture and chicken broth. Bring to a boil and cook, stirring, until mixture thickens, about 3 minutes. (Sauce may separate and appear "watery," but it will smooth out as liquid reduces.) Return chicken to the skillet, with any accumulated juices, reduce heat to low, and simmer until completely heated through, 3 to 4 minutes.

6. Place cooked pasta in a large, shallow serving bowl and top with the chicken mixture. Garnish with fresh basil sprigs.

Serves 4

Holiday Chicken with Apples and Cranberries

Exciting holiday colors spark our imaginations, as shown by this tempting chicken dish. Add broccoli florets and wild rice pilaf to the plate for an artful presentation.

4	fresh or frozen skinless, boneless chicken breast halves
	Salt and pepper
1/2	tablespoon vegetable oil
1/2	tablespoon unsalted butter
1	firm, unpeeled green apple, cored, sliced, and drizzled with lemon juice
1/2	cup fresh cranberries
1/2	cup low-salt chicken broth, canned or homemade (page 177)
1	tablespoon brandy
1	tablespoon sugar
1/2	teaspoon cinnamon
1/4	teaspoon ground allspice
1	teaspoon cornstarch, dissolved in 2 teaspoons water

1. For fresh chicken, go to step 2. If chicken breasts are frozen, place in a sealed plastic bag and thaw in a large pan of cold water for about 30 minutes or until flexible. Blot with paper towels.

2. Trim fresh or thawed breasts of any visible fat, and sprinkle lightly with salt and pepper. In a large, nonstick skillet, heat oil and butter over medium heat, and cook breasts, turning 2 to 3 times, until lightly browned, 4 to 5 minutes total. Remove breasts to a plate. To the skillet, add the sliced apples

and cook, stirring frequently until barely tender, 2 to 3 minutes. Add remaining ingredients. Stir and bring to a boil. Return breasts to the skillet. Reduce heat to medium-low and simmer, uncovered, turning the breasts 2 to 3 times, until sauce is thickened and cranberries pop, 6 to 8 minutes. Taste sauce and adjust seasoning, if needed.

Serves 4

Chicken with Hot and Sweet Peppers

Large, thick-meated jalapeño chile peppers are very popular and are now widely available during most of the year. This healthy chicken dish is a bit spicy and is visually exciting when topped with colorful green, red, and yellow peppers. Jalapeños vary in heat, so use the amount that suits you.

4	fresh or frozen skinless, boneless chicken breast halves
3	tablespoons olive oil
	Salt and pepper
2	to 4 large jalapeño chiles, seeded and cut into $1/8$-inch strips
$1/2$	large red bell pepper, seeded and cut into $1/8$-inch strips
$1/2$	large yellow bell pepper, seeded and cut into $1/8$-inch strips
1	garlic clove, minced
1	tablespoon fresh lemon juice

1. For fresh chicken, go to step 2. If chicken breasts are frozen, place in sealed plastic bag and thaw in a large pan of cold water about 30 to 35 minutes or until flexible. Blot with paper towels.

2. Trim fresh or thawed breasts of any visible fat. In a large, nonstick skillet, heat oil over medium heat. Add breasts, and sprinkle lightly with salt and pepper. Cook until golden brown, 4 to 5 minutes. Turn and cook second side another 4 minutes or until meat is white throughout in the thickest

part but still juicy. Transfer breasts to a warmed serving platter. In the same skillet, cook the jalapeños, red and yellow peppers, and garlic, stirring, until barely tender, about 3 minutes. Stir in the lemon juice and spoon the peppers over the chicken. Serve.

Serves 4

Chicken Kebabs

*Skewered chicken is a treat anytime. Middle Eastern season-
ings make these kebabs spicy and flavorful. For the best flavor,
chicken should marinate for several hours.*

4	fresh or frozen skinless, boneless chicken breast halves
1/2	teaspoon salt
2	garlic cloves, pressed
1	teaspoon Hungarian paprika
1/2	teaspoon cinnamon
1/4	teaspoon ground allspice
1/8	teaspoon cayenne
1/4	cup fresh lemon juice
3	tablespoons plain yogurt, lowfat or regular
2	tablespoons olive oil
1/4	teaspoon pepper
1	green or red bell pepper, seeded and cut into 1 1/2-inch pieces
4	(10-inch) wooden skewers, soaked in water

1. For fresh chicken breasts, go to step 2. If breasts are
   frozen, place in a sealed plastic bag and thaw in a large
   pan of cold water about 35 minutes or until flexible. Blot
   with paper towels.

2. Trim fresh or thawed breasts of any visible fat, and cut into
   neat 1 1/2-inch pieces. Place in a medium, nonreactive
   bowl. Set aside. In another medium bowl, mash together
   salt, garlic, paprika, cinnamon, allspice, and cayenne. Add
   lemon juice, yogurt, olive oil, and pepper. Combine well.
   Add to the bowl with chicken. Toss to coat the pieces with
   the marinade. Cover and refrigerate 2 to 6 hours.

3. Shortly before cooking, prepare a hot fire in a barbecue grill. Skewer the chicken pieces alternately with the bell pepper pieces, using 4 pieces of chicken and 3 pieces of pepper per skewer. Place on a hot, oiled grill rack and grill 5 to 6 minutes, turning and basting with the marinade, until the chicken is golden and white throughout. Serve with rice.

Serves 4

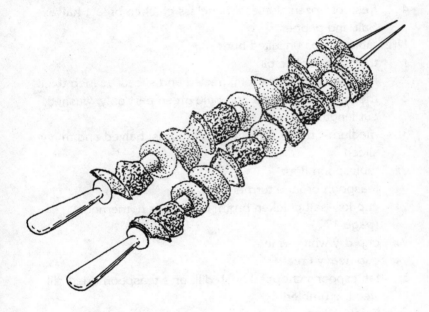

Chicken with Leeks, Carrots, and Mushrooms

Here's a first-rate entree with a creamy dill-flavored sauce that's simple, quick, and elegant enough for entertaining.

4	fresh or frozen skinless, boneless chicken breast halves
	Salt and pepper
1 1/2	tablespoons unsalted butter
1	tablespoon olive oil
2	medium slender carrots, peeled and sliced 1/8 inch thick
2	medium leeks, white and pale green part only, washed, cut lengthwise, and sliced
8	medium Crimini (brown) mushrooms, halved and thinly sliced
1/2	tablespoon flour
1/4	teaspoon ground turmeric
3/4	cup low-salt chicken broth, canned or homemade (page 177)
1/4	cup dry white wine
1/4	cup heavy cream
2	tablespoons chopped fresh dill, or 1 teaspoon dried dill weed, crumbled
	Fresh dill sprigs

1. For fresh chicken, go to step 2. If breasts are frozen, to thaw quickly, rinse under cold running water for 3 to 5 minutes or until flexible. Blot with paper towels.

2. Trim fresh or thawed breasts of any visible fat. Place breasts between two sheets of plastic wrap and pound with flat side of a meat mallet or a rolling pin to an even thick-

ness of 1/4 inch. Sprinkle breasts lightly with salt and pepper. In a large, nonstick skillet, heat 1/2 tablespoon of the butter with the oil. Cook chicken, turning, until light brown on both sides and white throughout, 6 to 8 minutes total. Transfer to a plate.

3. In the same skillet, add remaining 1 tablespoon of butter over medium heat. Add carrots, leeks, and mushrooms. Cook, stirring frequently, until vegetables begin to color, about 5 minutes. Stir in flour and turmeric. Cook, stirring, 1 minute. Add broth, wine, cream, and dill. Cover and cook until vegetables are tender and sauce has thickened slightly, 6 to 8 minutes. Return chicken and accumulated juices to the skillet. Heat through, over medium-low heat, for about 3 to 4 minutes. Season to taste with salt and pepper. Serve chicken with sauce and vegetables spooned over the pieces. Garnish with fresh dill sprigs.

Serves 4

Sautéed Chicken Breasts with Lentils

Winter vegetables cooked with nutritious lentils and topped with a boneless chicken breast make a satisfying cold weather meal.

4	fresh or frozen skinless, boneless chicken breast halves
1 1/2	cups dried lentils
2	bay leaves
1/2	teaspoon dried oregano
3	tablespoons olive oil
1/2	medium onion, finely chopped
2	large garlic cloves, finely chopped
2	medium carrots, peeled and cut into 1/4-inch cubes
1	medium turnip, peeled and cut into 1/4-inch cubes
1/2	medium green bell pepper, seeded and cut into 1/4-inch cubes
1/2	cup low-salt chicken broth, canned or homemade (page 177)
	Salt and pepper
2	tablespoons chopped fresh parsley

1. For fresh chicken, go to step 2. If chicken breasts are frozen, to thaw quickly, rinse under cold running water 3 to 5 minutes or until flexible. Blot with paper towels.

2. Trim fresh or thawed breasts of any visible fat. Place the breasts on a plate, cover, and refrigerate until ready to cook.

3. Put lentils in a wire strainer and rinse well. Place in a large saucepan with bay leaf and oregano. Cover with water by

2 inches. Bring to a boil over high heat. Reduce heat to medium-low and simmer, uncovered, 25 to 30 minutes until tender. Drain, but do not rinse. Remove bay leaf. Reserve in the pan, off heat.

4. Meanwhile, in a medium skillet, heat 1 1/2 tablespoons of the olive oil over medium heat and cook onion and garlic, stirring, until onion is translucent, about 3 minutes. Add carrots, turnip, green pepper, and chicken broth. Stir to combine. Bring to a boil, then reduce heat to medium-low, cover, and cook until carrots and turnips are barely tender, 3 to 4 minutes. Combine with cooked lentils and keep warm over low heat.

5. In a large, nonstick skillet, heat remaining 1 1/2 tablespoons olive oil over medium-high heat. Add chicken breasts, sprinkle with salt and pepper, and sauté until lightly browned and white throughout, 3 to 4 minutes on each side.

6. To serve, divide heated lentils and vegetables equally in centers of four serving plates, and top each serving with one chicken breast. Sprinkle with parsley.

Serves 4

Chicken with Thai Jasmine Rice and Mangos

This plate explodes with color and flavor excitement. Thai Jasmine rice can be found in Asian specialty shops or in the oriental section of many supermarkets.

4	fresh or frozen skinless, boneless chicken breast halves
2	tablespoons vegetable oil
1	medium onion, halved lengthwise and thinly sliced crosswise
1	red bell pepper, halved lengthwise and sliced crosswise
1	garlic clove, minced
4	thin fresh ginger slices
	Salt and pepper
1/4	cup low-salt chicken broth, canned or homemade (page 177)
2	tablespoons soy sauce
1	large ripe mango, peeled and sliced
20	thin fresh whole green beans, cooked *al dente*, about 6 minutes
2	cups hot, cooked Thai Jasmine rice
	Chutney (optional)

1. For fresh chicken, go to step 2. If chicken breasts are frozen, to thaw quickly, rinse under cold running water 3 to 5 minutes or until flexible. Blot with paper towels.

2. Trim fresh or thawed chicken of any visible fat, and cut into 1-inch pieces. Set aside. In a large, nonstick skillet, heat oil over medium heat and cook onion, red pepper, garlic, and

ginger, stirring, until vegetables are crisp-tender, about 2 minutes. Transfer to a medium bowl and reserve.

3. Add chicken to the same skillet. Season with salt and pepper. Cook, turning, until lightly browned, 3 to 4 minutes. Add broth, soy sauce, and the reserved vegetables. Bring to a boil. Remove from heat. Discard ginger slices.

4. To serve, arrange mango slices and cooked green beans on the outside edges of four serving plates. Pack 1/2 cup rice into a small bowl or custard cup, and invert to make a dome in center of each plate. Spoon chicken and vegetables around the rice domes. Serve at once. Pass the chutney.

Serves 4

Chicken Parmesan

*Serve this popular Italian-style dish with orzo pasta, green
salad, and garlic bread for a reliable and easy meal that's
always greeted with pleasure.*

4	fresh or frozen skinless, boneless chicken breast halves
2	tablespoons flour
1/2	teaspoon salt
1/8	teaspoon pepper
3	tablespoons olive oil
2 1/2	cups prepared marinara sauce, bottled or homemade
1/4	cup dry red wine
1	cup (4 ounces) shredded mozzarella cheese
1/4	cup shredded Parmesan cheese
	Fresh basil sprigs

1. For fresh chicken, go to step 2. If chicken breasts are
   frozen, place in a sealed plastic bag and thaw in a large pan
   of cold water 25 to 30 minutes or until flexible. Blot with
   paper towels.

2. Trim fresh or thawed breasts of any visible fat. Place each
   breast between two sheets of plastic wrap and pound with
   flat side of a meat mallet or a rolling pin to an even thickness of 1/4 inch. In a pie plate, combine flour, salt, and pepper. Dredge breasts in flour mixture to coat. Shake off
   excess flour and place breasts on a platter.

3. In a large skillet, heat the oil over medium heat. Add
   chicken and cook, turning, until golden, 3 to 4 minutes on
   each side. Transfer breasts to a platter. Discard oil from the
   skillet. Add the marinara sauce and wine. (If sauce is too
   thick, add water 1 tablespoon at a time to reach desired

consistency.) Bring sauce to a boil, then reduce heat to low and lay chicken in the skillet in one layer. Spoon a thin coating of sauce over the breasts. Divide mozzarella evenly over the centers of each breast. Sprinkle each with Parmesan. Cover the skillet and cook over low heat for 3 to 4 minutes or until cheese is melted and sauce is bubbling.

4. To serve, carefully lift breasts with a wide spatula, one at a time, and place in centers of four serving plates. Without covering the melted cheese toppings, spoon remaining sauce evenly around each serving. Garnish with fresh basil sprigs.

Serves 4

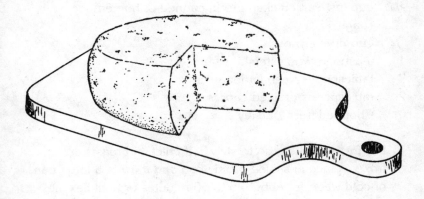

Piccata Style Chicken with Capers and Lemon

To make this popular Italian dish quickly, whether using fresh or frozen chicken, pound the breasts ahead of time. Cover and refrigerate until ready to cook. Time at the stove is really minimal.

4	fresh or frozen skinless, boneless chicken breast halves
	Salt and freshly ground black pepper
2	tablespoons olive oil
1	tablespoon unsalted butter
1/2	tablespoon flour
3/4	cup low-salt chicken broth, canned or homemade (page 177)
1/4	cup dry vermouth
1	teaspoon Worcestershire sauce
3	tablespoons fresh lemon juice
2	tablespoons drained capers
	Chopped fresh parsley

1. For fresh chicken, go to step 2. If chicken breasts are frozen, place in sealed plastic bag and thaw in a large pan of cold water for about 25 to 30 minutes or until flexible.

2. Trim any visible fat from fresh or thawed breasts. Pat dry with paper towels. Place one breast at a time between two sheets of plastic wrap and pound with flat side of a meat mallet or a rolling pin to an even thickness of about 1/4 inch. Sprinkle breasts lightly with salt and pepper.

3. In a large, nonstick skillet, heat oil and butter over medium-high heat. Add chicken and cook until lightly browned, 3 to

4 minutes. Turn and cook until just firm to the touch, about 2 minutes. Remove breasts to a warm platter. Stir flour into pan drippings and cook 1 minute. Add broth, vermouth, and Worcestershire sauce to skillet. Bring to a boil and cook, stirring, until slightly thickened and reduced by about one-third. Stir in lemon juice and capers. Season to taste with salt.

4. To serve, place one chicken breast on each of four serving plates. Pour sauce from the skillet equally over each serving. Sprinkle with chopped parsley. Serve hot.

Serves 4

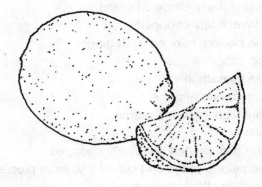

Chicken Breasts with Summer Plum Chutney

The abundant fresh plums of summer make a wonderful fresh chutney. The sauce is so easy and delicious that it may become a summertime favorite.

4 fresh or frozen skinless, boneless chicken breasts halves
2 1/2 tablespoons olive oil
Salt and pepper
1/2 cup sugar
1/4 cup red wine vinegar
1/4 cup unseasoned rice vinegar
2 tablespoons finely chopped onion
1 garlic clove, finely chopped
1 teaspoon peeled, minced fresh ginger
1/4 teaspoon salt
1/4 teaspoon cinnamon
1/4 teaspoon ground allspice
1/8 teaspoon freshly ground nutmeg
1/4 cup raisins
1 jalapeño chile, seeded and finely chopped
4 fresh red plums, pitted and cut into 1/2-inch pieces
Fresh basil or cilantro sprigs

1. For fresh chicken, go to step 2. If chicken breasts are frozen, place in a sealed plastic bag, and thaw in a large pan of cold water 25 to 30 minutes or until flexible. Blot with paper towels.

2. Trim fresh or thawed breasts of any visible fat. Rub breasts with about 1/2 tablespoon of the olive oil and sprinkle lightly

with salt and pepper. Cover and refrigerate until shortly before cooking.

3. In a medium, nonreactive saucepan, place sugar, vinegars, onion, garlic, ginger, salt, cinnamon, allspice, and nutmeg. Bring to a boil over medium-high heat, stirring, and cook until sugar dissolves, about 1 minute. Add raisins and jalapeño. Reduce heat to medium-low and simmer until juices begin to thicken, 4 to 5 minutes. Add plums and simmer, stirring frequently, until plums are tender but still hold their shapes. With a slotted spoon, lift solids out of the pan and place in a medium bowl. Bring remaining juices in the pan to a boil and cook, stirring frequently, until reduced to a shiny syrup, 3 to 4 minutes. Pour syrup into the bowl with the plum mixture and combine. Cool to room temperature, then cover and refrigerate until shortly before serving. Chutney can be made up to 5 days in advance.

4. In a medium, nonstick skillet, heat remaining 2 tablespoons of the olive oil over medium heat. Add chicken breasts and cook until lightly browned, about 4 minutes. Turn and cook 3 to 4 minutes more or until white throughout but still juicy. Reheat chutney. Serve chicken with a strip of plum chutney spooned over the centers of each chicken breast. Garnish with fresh basil or cilantro sprigs.

Serves 4

Sautéed Chicken with Baby Peas and Prosciutto

An eye-catching dish worthy of a special dinner party. Roasted red new potatoes are a natural partner.

4	fresh or frozen skinless, boneless chicken breast halves
2	tablespoons olive oil
1	package (10 ounces) frozen tiny peas, thawed
1	garlic clove, pressed
1	ounce prosciutto, cut into thin strips
2	tablespoons unsalted butter
	Salt and pepper
1	teaspoon flour
1/3	cup low-salt chicken broth, canned or homemade (page 177)
2	tablespoons fresh lemon juice
2	tablespoons chopped fresh parsley

1. For fresh chicken, go to step 2. If chicken breasts are frozen, place in sealed plastic bag and thaw in a large pan of cold water 25 to 30 minutes or until flexible. Blot with paper towels.

2. Trim fresh or thawed chicken of any visible fat. Place breasts between two sheets of plastic wrap and pound with flat side of a meat mallet or a rolling pin to an even thickness of 1/4 inch. Set aside.

3. In a large, nonstick skillet, heat oil over medium heat. Add peas, garlic, and prosciutto. Cook, stirring, until peas are barely tender, 1 to 2 minutes. Transfer to a bowl, scraping out bits of garlic and prosciutto.

4. In the same skillet, heat the butter over medium heat. Sprinkle chicken lightly with salt and pepper. Sauté chicken on both sides until very lightly browned, 4 to 6 minutes. Remove breasts to a plate. Stir flour into the skillet. Add broth, lemon juice, and parsley. Stirring rapidly, bring to a boil. Reduce heat to low and return chicken to the pan. Turn to coat with sauce. Add the peas and prosciutto. Heat through and serve at once.

Serves 4

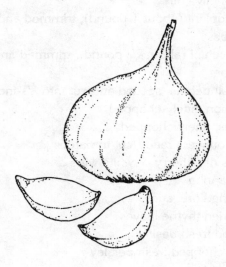

Chicken with Ratatouille

To shorten cooking time, this ratatouille version cuts the vegetables into small cubes, which makes an attractive bed for the sautéed chicken strips. Add crusty bread, and you have a nourishing meal.

12	fresh or frozen chicken breast tenders (about 12 ounces)
4	tablespoons olive oil
1	medium eggplant (about 1 pound), trimmed and cut into 1/3-inch cubes
3	medium zucchini (about 3/4 pound), trimmed and cut into 1/3-inch cubes
1/2	large red bell pepper, seeded and cut into 1/3-inch dices
1/2	medium onion, finely chopped
2	garlic cloves, finely chopped
1	can (14 1/2 ounces) ready-cut tomatoes
1	tablespoons dry sherry or white wine
1	teaspoon paprika
1/2	teaspoon dried oregano
1/2	teaspoon dried thyme leaves
1/4	cup chopped fresh basil
1	tablespoon chopped fresh parsley
	Juice of 1/2 lemon
	Salt and pepper to taste

1. For fresh chicken tenders, go to step 2. If chicken tenders are frozen, thaw in sealed plastic bag in a large pan of cold water for 15 to 20 minutes or until moist and flexible. Blot with paper towels.

2. Remove any thick white tendons from fresh or thawed chicken breast tenders. Place tenders on a plate, cover, and refrigerate until ready to cook.

3. In a large, heavy saucepan, heat 2 tablespoons of the oil over medium-high heat. Add eggplant and cook, tossing, until it begins to soften and moisture appears, about 3 minutes. Add zucchini, red pepper, onion, and garlic. Cook, stirring, another 2 minutes. Reduce heat to medium-low and add tomatoes, sherry, paprika, oregano, and thyme. Cover and cook, stirring frequently, until vegetables are tender, 10 to 12 minutes. Stir in basil, parsley, and lemon juice. Season to taste with salt and pepper. (Can be made 1 day ahead to this point. Cover and refrigerate until ready to use.) Reheat about 20 minutes before serving.

4. Heat remaining 2 tablespoons oil in a large, nonstick skillet over medium heat. Add chicken tenders and sprinkle lightly with salt and pepper. Sauté the tenders, turning, until lightly browned and white throughout, 5 to 6 minutes.

5. To serve, spoon the hot ratatouille onto a large platter. Arrange chicken tenders over the vegetables and serve. Garnish with sprigs of fresh basil, if desired.

Serves 4

Chicken Sauté with Braised Red Chard

Red chard is an American classic vegetable that has regained popularity. It goes very well with chicken. The beautiful color of the chard holds well through cooking, and it retains good texture if not overcooked. The chard can be prepared ahead of time, then reheated shortly before serving. For a hearty entree, add oven-roasted new potatoes to complete the plate.

Chard:

2	bunches red chard, washed very well
2	tablespoons olive oil
1	medium onion, peeled and chopped
3	garlic cloves, chopped
1/4	cup red wine vinegar
2	teaspoons sugar
	Salt and freshly ground black pepper

1. Cut all but about 2 inches of the red stems off the chard and discard. Cut remaining stems and leaves crosswise into 1/2-inch pieces. Place in a heavy, large, nonreactive saucepan with 1/2 cup water. Cook, uncovered, over medium-high heat, stirring frequently, for 10 to 12 minutes or until barely tender. Transfer to a large, nonreactive bowl. Sprinkle with salt and set aside.

2. Rinse and dry the pan. Heat oil over medium heat. Add onion and garlic. Cook, stirring frequently, until onion begins to brown, about 4 minutes. Add vinegar and sugar. Stir to combine and dissolve sugar. Return chard to the pan.

Toss to combine. Season to taste with salt and freshly ground black pepper. Partially cover the pan and cook over low heat for 5 minutes. Set aside.

Chicken:

4   fresh or frozen skinless, boneless chicken breast halves
      Salt and pepper
2   tablespoons olive oil
      Chopped fresh parsley

1. For fresh chicken, go to step 2. If breasts are frozen, to thaw quickly, rinse under cold running water for 3 to 5 minutes or until flexible. Blot with paper towels.

2. Trim fresh or thawed breasts of any visible fat. Sprinkle breasts with salt and pepper. In a large, nonstick skillet, heat oil over medium heat. When oil shimmers, add chicken and cook, turning, until lightly browned on both sides and white throughout, 8 to 10 minutes total. Reheat chard, if needed. Divide chard equally among four serving plates. Top each serving with one chicken breast. Sprinkle chicken with parsley. Add roasted potatoes, if desired.

Serves 4

Braised Chicken
with Rosemary

Rosemary with chicken is a classic marriage. To get the best flavor and succulence from this dish, use fresh chicken breast halves with rib bones attached, or if using frozen chicken, thaw it overnight in the refrigerator. Fresh sprigs of rosemary are preferred, but dried rosemary leaves can be used as well.

2   tablespoons olive oil
1   tablespoon unsalted butter
4   fresh or thawed chicken breast halves, on the bone
     Salt and pepper
2   garlic cloves, chopped
     Chopped leaves of 1 small branch fresh rosemary or
     $1/2$ teaspoon dried rosemary
$1/2$ cup dry white wine
$1/2$ cup low-salt chicken broth, canned or homemade
     (page 177)

In a heavy, deep skillet, heat oil and butter over medium-high heat. When foam subsides, add chicken breast, skin side down, and cook until golden brown, about 3 minutes. Reduce heat to medium-low, turn breasts over, sprinkle with salt and pepper, and cook the second side for 1 minute. Add garlic and rosemary. Stir gently to coat with oil, and cook 1 minute more. Add the wine and chicken broth. Cover and simmer over low heat, turning the chicken 2 or 3 times, for 15–18 minutes or until meat is white throughout. Serve with the pan juices.

Serves 4

Speedy Grilled Chicken with Garlic, Mint, and Mangos

For an informal outdoor meal, serve this quick and lively flavored grilled chicken with juicy golden mangos. Add tossed greens and rice or pasta salad.

2	ripe mangos, peeled and thinly sliced
4	fresh or frozen skinless, boneless chicken breast halves
3	tablespoons olive oil
2	large garlic cloves, minced
1	tablespoon red wine vinegar
1	tablespoon minced fresh mint
1	teaspoon soy sauce
1/2	teaspoon salt
1/4	teaspoon pepper

1. Arrange sliced mangos on a serving platter, cover, and re-frigerate until shortly before serving. Prepare a hot fire in a barbecue grill. Oil the grill.

2. For fresh chicken, go to step 3. If chicken breasts are frozen, to thaw quickly, rinse under cold running water about 3 to 5 minutes or until flexible. Blot with paper towels and place on a nonreactive platter in a single layer.

3. In a small bowl, mix olive oil, garlic, vinegar, mint, soy sauce, salt, and pepper. Spoon mint mixture on the chicken. Turn to coat well. Let stand 30 minutes. When coals are hot, scrape excess marinade off chicken. Place chicken on oiled grill over hot coals and grill, 4 to 5 minutes on each side or until chicken is white throughout but still juicy. Serve with mangos.

Serves 4

Russian Walnut Chicken

From the Georgia region of Russia, known for its fine cooking, comes this interpretation of chicken prepared with crunchy walnuts and aromatic spices. During fall or winter, try sprinkling pomegranate seeds over the finished dish.

4	fresh or frozen skinless, boneless chicken breast halves
	Salt and pepper
1/4	cup flour
1	tablespoon unsalted butter
1	tablespoon vegetable oil
1/2	medium onion, finely chopped
2	garlic cloves, minced
1/2	cup finely chopped walnuts
3/4	cup low-salt chicken broth, canned or homemade (page 177)
1	tablespoon white wine vinegar
1/4	teaspoon cinnamon
1/4	teaspoon ground allspice
1/4	teaspoon turmeric
1/8	teaspoon freshly ground nutmeg
1	tablespoon minced fresh parsley
	Walnut pieces for garnish

1. For fresh chicken, go to step 2. If breasts are frozen, place in a sealed plastic bag and thaw in a large pan of cold water for 25 to 30 minutes or until flexible. Blot with paper towels.

2. Trim fresh or thawed breasts of any visible fat. Sprinkle lightly with salt and pepper. Dust the breasts with flour and shake off excess. In a large, nonstick skillet, heat butter and

oil over medium heat and cook chicken, turning, until lightly browned on both sides and white throughout but still juicy, 8 to 10 minutes total (depending upon the thickness of the breasts). Remove to a platter and keep warm.

3. In the same skillet, cook onion, garlic, and chopped walnuts, stirring, until onions are softened, about 3 minutes. Sprinkle 1/2 tablespoon of the flour used to dust the chicken over the onion mixture, and cook, stirring, 1 minute. Add chicken broth, vinegar, and spices. Cook, stirring frequently, until sauce thickens and flavors blend, 4 to 5 minutes. Return chicken pieces to the skillet along with any accumulated juices, and simmer over low heat for 2 minutes. Season to taste with salt and freshly ground black pepper.

4. Place one breast on each of four serving plates and spoon sauce over the chicken. Sprinkle with parsley and walnut pieces.

Serves 4

Chicken Tenders with Spanish Saffron Rice, Carrot Shreds, and Asparagus

This pretty dish with its yellow hues is perfect for a spring meal. Fresh asparagus adds color and texture to complete the plate. Frozen chicken breast tenders thaw while the rice cooks.

12	fresh or frozen chicken breast tenders (about 12 ounces)
2	tablespoons unsalted butter
1/2	small onion, finely chopped
1/8	teaspoon crumbled Spanish saffron threads
1 1/2	cups long-grain rice
2 3/4	cups low-salt chicken broth, canned or homemade (page 177)
1/2	cup shredded carrot
1/4	teaspoon salt
1/8	teaspoon white pepper
2	tablespoons olive oil
1/2	teaspoon paprika
	Chopped fresh parsley
	Cooked asparagus spears

1. For fresh chicken, go to step 2. If chicken tenders are frozen, place in a sealed plastic bag and thaw in a large pan of cold water for about 20 to 25 minutes or until flexible. Blot with paper towels.

2. Cut fresh or thawed chicken tenders in half, lengthwise, and set aside.

3. In a heavy, medium saucepan, heat butter over medium heat and cook onion, stirring, until it softens, about 3 min-

utes. Stir in saffron and rice. Cook, stirring, another 2 minutes. Add broth, raise heat, and bring to a brisk boil, uncovered; then reduce heat to low, cover, and cook until liquid is absorbed and rice is tender, about 18 minutes.

Remove pan from heat and carefully stir in shredded carrot, salt, and white pepper. Cover and let rice stand 5 minutes.

4. Meanwhile, in a medium, nonstick skillet, heat oil over medium-high heat and sauté chicken tenders, turning, until lightly browned and white throughout, about 4 minutes. Season to taste with salt and sprinkle with paprika. Toss to distribute the seasonings. Transfer rice to a warmed serving platter. Arrange chicken over the rice. Sprinkle with parsley and serve with asparagus.

Serves 4

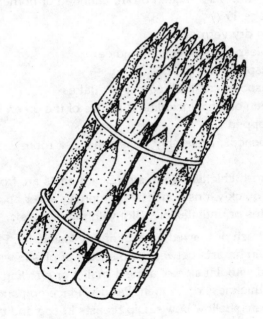

Chicken Scallops
with Avocado

Boneless chicken breasts are pounded, sautéed, and gently braised in broth and vermouth, then served with creamy avocado slices for an unusual and flavorful entree. Orzo pasta or steamed rice go well with the chicken and avocado.

4	fresh or frozen skinless, boneless chicken breast halves
1	well-beaten egg
1/2	cup flour
2	tablespoons vegetable oil
1	tablespoon unsalted butter
3/4	cup low-salt chicken broth, cannned or homemade (page 177)
1/4	cup dry vermouth
2	tablespoons fresh lemon juice
1/2	teaspoon salt
1/8	teaspoon crushed red pepper flakes
2	green onions, including 2 inches of the green, finely chopped
2	avocados, preferably Hass variety, at room temperature

1. For fresh chicken, go to step 2. If breasts are frozen, to thaw quickly, rinse under cold running water about 3 to 5 minutes or until flexible. Blot with paper towels.

2. Trim fresh or thawed breasts of any visible fat. Place chicken breasts between two sheets of plastic wrap and pound with flat side of a meat mallet or a rolling pin to an even thickness of 1/4 inch. Pat dry. Place egg and flour in separate shallow bowls. Dip breasts in egg and then dust

with flour. In a large, nonstick skillet, heat oil and butter over medium heat and sauté chicken breasts, two at a time, until lightly browned, about 3 minutes on each side. Transfer breasts, as they are cooked, to a platter.

3. When all chicken pieces are browned, add to the skillet the broth, vermouth, 1 tablespoon of the lemon juice, salt, and pepper flakes. Bring to a boil, stirring. Return the chicken pieces and accumulated juices to the skillet with the sauce. Spoon sauce over the chicken, and sprinkle evenly with green onions. Simmer over low heat, basting breasts several times with the sauce until completely heated through, about 5 minutes.

4. Meanwhile, peel and slice each avocado into 8 even slices. Sprinkle with remaining 1 tablespoon of the lemon juice. Arrange the chicken and avocados on each of four serving plates. Spoon sauce equally over the chicken on each plate and serve.

Serves 4

Chicken Schnitzel

Although this dish is usually made with thin veal cutlets, chicken breasts make terrific schnitzels.

4	fresh or frozen skinless, boneless chicken breast halves
	Salt and pepper
1/2	cup flour
2	eggs
1	cup fine dry bread crumbs
4	tablespoons vegetable oil
	Chopped fresh parsley
	Lemon wedges

1. For fresh chicken, go to step 2. If chicken breasts are frozen, place in a sealed plastic bag and thaw in a large pan of cold water for about 30 minutes or until flexible. Blot with paper towels.

2. Trim fresh or thawed breasts of any visible fat. Place between two pieces of plastic wrap and pound with flat side of a meat mallet or a rolling pin to an even thickness of 1/8 inch. Pat breasts dry with paper towels and sprinkle lightly with salt and pepper. Set aside.

3. Put the flour on a sheet of waxed paper. In a medium bowl, beat the eggs with 2 tablespoons of water. Put the bread crumbs on a pie plate. Dust each chicken breast lightly with flour, then dip each breast in the egg mixture and coat both sides with bread crumbs. Place the chicken breasts in a single layer on a large platter and refrigerate 20 to 30 minutes.

4. In a large, nonstick skillet, heat 2 tablespoons of the oil over medium-high heat. When the oil shimmers, add two of the breasts and cook until golden brown, 2 to 3 minutes. Turn and cook until golden and white throughout, 1 to 2 minutes. Drain on paper towels. Wipe the skillet clean. Heat remaining 2 tablespoons oil and cook remaining two breasts. Sprinkle the chicken with parsley. Serve with lemon wedges.

Serves 4

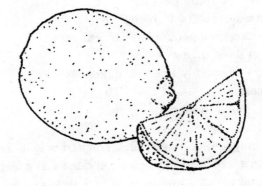

Sicilian Red Devil Chicken

A deep red sauce with a touch of spice makes a devilishly good chicken dish. For a lively color contrast, serve over green pasta.

4	fresh or frozen skinless, boneless chicken breast halves
	Salt and pepper
3	tablespoons olive oil
1	medium onion, chopped
3	large garlic cloves, minced
1	can (14 1/2 ounces) ready-cut tomatoes
3	tablespoons tomato paste
1/2	cup red wine, such as Chianti
2	tablespoons chopped Italian flat-leaf parsley
1/2	teaspoon dried thyme
1/4	teaspoon crushed red pepper flakes
2	bay leaves
	Spinach pasta (optional)

1. For fresh chicken, go to step 2. If chicken breasts are frozen, place in sealed plastic bag and thaw in a large pan of cold water about 35 minutes or until flexible. Blot with paper towels.

2. Trim fresh or thawed chicken breasts of any visible fat, and cut each breast into three equal pieces. Sprinkle lightly with salt and pepper. In a heavy, large saucepan, heat oil over medium heat and cook the chicken pieces, in batches, without crowding, until lightly browned on both sides. Transfer breast pieces to a bowl. (Chicken will not be

cooked through.) To the saucepan, add the onion and garlic. Cook, stirring, until onion is translucent, about 3 minutes. Add remaining ingredients and bring to a boil. Return
chicken to the pan, reduce heat to low, cover, and simmer
for about 12 to 15 minutes for flavors to blend. Remove
bay leaves and serve over spinach pasta if desired.

Serves 4

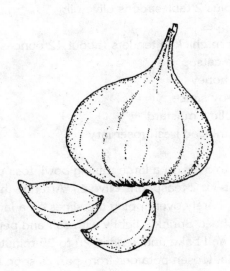

Skillet Chicken and Potatoes with Honey Mustard and Rosemary

This is a favorite for potato lovers, and it's so easy, you'll want to serve it often.

4   uniform medium new potatoes, scrubbed and sliced
        1/4 inch thick
2   teaspoons plus 2 tablespoons olive oil
        Salt and pepper
12   fresh or frozen chicken tenders (about 12 ounces)
2   tablespoons catsup
1   tablespoon honey
3   teaspoons soy sauce
1   teaspoon yellow mustard
1/2   tablespoon minced fresh rosemary

1. Preheat oven to 375°. In a large mixing bowl, toss potatoes to coat with about 2 teaspoons olive oil. Arrange the potato slices in rows, barely overlapping the slices on a large foil-lined baking sheet. Sprinkle lightly with salt and pepper. Place in oven and bake until tender, 20 to 25 minutes. With a small spatula, loosen potatoes from pan as soon as they are done to prevent sticking.

2. Meanwhile, cut each fresh or frozen chicken tender into two equal pieces, and place tenders on a platter. (Frozen tenders will thaw while the potatoes bake.) Set aside.

3. In a medium bowl, combine catsup, honey, soy sauce, and mustard. Set aside.

4. In a large, nonstick skillet, heat 2 tablespoons olive oil over medium heat and cook chicken tenders, turning, until lightly browned, 4 to 5 minutes. Add the potatoes and the sauce. Stir to coat potatoes and chicken with the sauce. Add rosemary. Cook, stirring, until sizzling and heated through, 3 to 4 minutes.

Serves 4

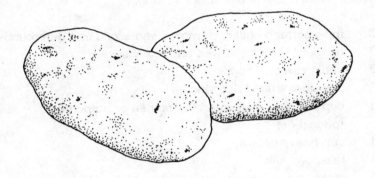

Southwestern Grilled Chicken Breasts with Serrano Sauce, Zucchini, Corn, and Red Peppers

This visually exciting and sophisticated dish needs only warm corn or flour tortillas to make a complete entree. Mexican-style black beans can be offered as a side dish. The spicy sauce is best if made a few hours before serving.

3	fresh serrano chiles, stemmed and sliced into thin rounds
3	medium shallots, halved and thinly sliced
3	garlic cloves, chopped
1/4	cup unseasoned rice vinegar
1	cup low-salt chicken broth, canned or homemade (page 177)
1	cup heavy cream
1	teaspoon salt
1	tablespoon olive oil plus additional for grilling
1	cup fresh (cut from about 2 ears) or frozen corn kernels
1	cup zucchini (about 4 ounces), cut into neat 1/4-inch cubes
1/2	medium red bell pepper, cut into neat 1/4-inch cubes
4	fresh or frozen skinless, boneless chicken breast halves
	Chopped fresh cilantro

1. In a medium, nonreactive saucepan, place serranos, shallots, garlic, and rice vinegar. Bring to a boil over medium-high heat, uncovered, until vinegar is reduced by half, 2 to 3 minutes. Add chicken broth and cream. Boil, stirring frequently, until sauce is reduced to about 1 cup and is thick

enough to coat the back of a wooden spoon, about 20 minutes. (Watch sauce carefully to avoid boiling over.) Strain sauce through a fine-mesh strainer into a medium bowl. Discard solids. Return sauce to pan. Season with 1/2 teaspoon of the salt. Cover and reserve.

2. In a medium skillet, heat olive oil over medium heat. Add corn, zucchini, and red pepper. Cook, tossing, until heated through and sizzling, 1 to 2 minutes. Reserve, off heat, in the pan.

3. Prepare a hot fire in a barbecue grill. For fresh chicken, go to step 4. If chicken breasts are frozen, to thaw quickly, rinse under cold running water 3 to 5 minutes or until flexible. Blot with paper towels.

4. Trim fresh or thawed breasts of any visible fat. Rub breasts all over with oil and sprinkle lightly with remaining 1/2 teaspoon salt. When coals are ready, oil the grill and place breasts on the rack set 4 to 6 inches from the coals. Grill about 4 minutes or until lightly browned, then turn and grill second side until breasts are just firm to the touch and white throughout but still juicy, 4 to 6 minutes. Transfer breasts to a warm platter, and reheat the reserved sauce and vegetables.

5. To serve, place one breast on each of four plates. Spoon heated sauce evenly over the breasts, letting some of the sauce pool onto the plates. Scatter the hot vegetables over all. Sprinkle each serving with chopped cilantro.

Serves 4

Chicken with Tomato, Wine, and Cream Sauce

When vine-ripened tomatoes are at their peak, make this elegant and easy sauce to serve with chicken breasts for a special-occasion meal. Frozen chicken breasts can thaw while making the sauce. Tiny baked or boiled new potatoes go very well with this dish. Complete the plate with bright green broccoli or fresh garden peas.

4	fresh or frozen skinless, boneless chicken breast halves
1	tablespoon olive oil
1	tablespoon butter
2	garlic cloves, minced
1	large shallot, minced
1/4	cup dry white wine
2	medium tomatoes, peeled, seeded, and finely chopped
3/4	cup heavy cream
	Salt and freshly ground black pepper
	Chopped fresh parsley

1. For fresh chicken, go to step 2. If chicken breasts are frozen, place in sealed plastic bag and thaw in a large pan of cold water for 25 to 30 minutes or until flexible. Blot with paper towels.

2. In a medium saucepan, heat 1/2 tablespoon of the oil and the butter over medium heat. Add garlic and shallot. Cook, stirring, until just beginning to brown, about 2 minutes. Add wine and cook, stirring, 1 minute. Add tomatoes, and raise heat to medium-high. Cook briskly until liquid is reduced by half, about 5 minutes. Add the cream. Reduce heat to

medium and cook, stirring frequently, until sauce thickens enough to coat the back of a spoon, 5 to 6 minutes. Season to taste with salt and freshly ground black pepper. Stir in parsley. Reserve off heat.

3. Trim fresh or thawed breasts of any visible fat. In a medium, nonstick skillet, heat remaining 1/2 tablespoon oil over medium heat. Add chicken. Sprinkle lightly with salt and pepper. Cook until golden brown, about 4 minutes. Turn and cook another 3 to 4 minutes or until white throughout. Reheat the sauce and serve over the chicken.

Serves 4

Braised Chicken with Prunes

Throughout the Mediterranean region, prunes are teamed with poultry and meats of all kinds. This Mediterranean inspiration shows how luscious the combination can be when made with boneless chicken breasts. Leaving the skin on helps prevent chicken from becoming too dry. Polenta is right at home with this dish.

4	fresh or frozen boneless chicken breasts, with skin
	Salt and freshly ground black pepper
3	tablespoons olive oil
1	medium onion, finely chopped
1	teaspoon Hungarian paprika
1/2	teaspoon dried oregano
1/2	teaspoon dried thyme leaves
3/4	cup low-salt chicken broth, canned or homemade (page 177)
1/3	cup dry red wine, such as Chianti
1	tablespoon tomato paste
12	pitted prunes
1	teaspoon orange zest
1	tablespoon chopped fresh parsley

1. For fresh chicken, go to step 2. If breasts are frozen, place in sealed plastic bag in a large pan of cold water and thaw 25 to 30 minutes or until flexible. Blot with paper towels.

2. Trim fresh or thawed breasts of excess fat, leaving most of the skin attached. Sprinkle with salt and pepper. In a large skillet, heat oil over medium-high heat. Add chicken, skin side down, and cook until golden brown, 3 to 4 minutes.

Turn and cook 1 minute. Chicken will not be cooked through. Transfer breasts to a plate and set aside.

3. To the same skillet, add onion and cook, stirring, until browned, 4 to 5 minutes. Add paprika, oregano, thyme, chicken broth, wine, tomato paste, prunes, and orange zest. Bring to a boil. Return chicken to the pan, skin side down, along with accumulated juices from the plate. Cover the pan, reduce heat to low and simmer 10 minutes. Turn chicken over and cook 10 minutes more. Transfer chicken and prunes to a warmed platter. Spoon juices over chicken. Sprinkle with parsley. Serve.

Serves 4

3

Let the Oven
Do the Cooking

Baking, broiling, or roasting chicken breast dishes in the oven allows freedom from constant attention, but they also require careful timing to ensure that the lean meat remains moist. Oven cooking often allows dishes to be partially prepared to a certain point, then covered and refrigerated until shortly before serving. Since chicken breasts cook at a high heat for a relatively short time, the final broiling, baking, or roasting means that these dishes will be ready in a hurry.

When chicken breasts are baked, broiled, or roasted, cooks must be aware that the breasts have very little internal fat and that dry-heat cooking requires certain precautions to avoid drying out the meat. To keep the chicken moist, it helps to bake or roast it on the bone with skin attached to seal in the natural juices. Baked chicken can also be coated with crumbs or some other covering to seal in juices. Extra moisture can be supplied by basting with oil, melted butter, or flavored liquids, such as broth, wine, or citrus juices.

Some of the dishes in this chapter call for cooking the chicken breasts covered with vegetables and other ingredients, in a moist environment, which creates its own sauce while cooking. Other recipes coat the breasts with seasoned crumbs, herbs, and spices to enhance flavor and seal in moisture while adding a crisp surface. Some of the recipes use a brushed-on glaze or call for stuffing, then roll the breasts in a coating for a delicious interior and a browned surface. There are lots of international flavors represented in this chapter, so be adventurous and try something new.

Baked Chicken with Mustard Crust

For this dish, fresh chicken breast halves with rib bones attached give the most succulent results. If the chicken is frozen, thaw it overnight in the refrigerator. The best crumb coating is achieved by using good whole-grain bread. Mashed garlic potatoes are a delicious partner with the chicken.

4   fresh or thawed chicken breast halves, on the bone
      Salt and pepper
1/4 cup olive oil
3   tablespoons country-style mustard
3/4 cup fresh bread crumbs, made from day-old whole-grain bread
1/3 cup grated Parmesan cheese
1/2 teaspoon paprika
1   tablespoon finely chopped fresh parsley

1. Preheat oven to 375°. Brush a 9 × 12-inch baking dish with oil. Trim excess fat and skin from chicken. Sprinkle breasts lightly with salt and pepper. Set aside.

2. In a medium mixing bowl, combine olive oil and mustard. In a pie plate, combine bread crumbs, cheese, paprika, and parsley. Spread skin sides of breasts with the mustard mixture, and pat on a thick coating of the crumb mixture. Place, crumb side up, in the baking pan, in a single layer. Cover with foil and bake about 25 minutes, then remove foil and continue baking another 15 minutes or until meat fork easily pierces the meat and juices run clear. Chicken will have a crisp brown crust and be juicy and tender inside. Serve hot.

Serves 4

Baked Chicken with Apricot Glaze and Cinnamon Couscous

A shiny apricot glaze flavors the chicken and helps to keep it moist while it bakes. For this recipe, use fresh chicken breasts on the bone or thaw frozen chicken overnight in the refrigerator. The accompanying couscous cooks quickly, by steeping in hot liquid. Look for couscous in the beans and rice section of supermarkets or in health food stores.

Chicken:

2 1/2 tablespoons apricot preserves
2   teaspoons vegetable oil
1   tablespoon red wine vinegar
1   teaspoon dry sherry
1/2   teaspoon dried thyme
4   fresh or thawed chicken breast halves, on the bone, with skin
       Salt and pepper

1. In a small saucepan, combine apricot preserves, 1 teaspoon of the vegetable oil, vinegar, sherry, and thyme. Bring to a boil, stirring, and cook until preserves are melted, about 1 minute.

2. Preheat oven to 400°. Trim fresh or thawed breasts of excess skin and fat, leaving a portion of skin intact. Rub chicken breasts with remainin 1 teaspoon of oil. Season lightly with salt and pepper. Place breasts in a shallow baking dish, skin side up in one layer, and bake for 15 minutes. Then brush chicken with apricot glaze and bake 20 to 25

minutes longer, brushing with glaze two more times, until skins are golden brown and meat is white throughout, and juices run clear when pierced with tip of sharp knife in the thickest part.

Couscous:

1	tablespoons olive oil
1/2	tablespoon unsalted butter
1 1/4	cups couscous
1 1/2	cups boiling water
1/4	teaspoon salt
1/2	teaspoon cinnamon
1/3	cup dried currants

While chicken bakes, in a medium saucepan heat oil and butter. Add couscous and cook, stirring, to coat the grains. Turn off heat. Add boiling water, salt, cinnamon, and currants. Stir to combine. Cover and let sit 15 to 20 minutes. Fluff with a fork and salt to taste. Serve with the chicken.

Serves 4

Chicken Breast with Artichoke Hearts and Black Olives

This terrific entree with lively Mediterranean flavors is inspired by Italian country cooking. Serve with orzo pasta and a simple mixed green salad.

4	fresh or frozen skinless, boneless chicken breast halves
3	tablespoons olive oil
1/2	medium onion, chopped
2	tablespoons finely chopped celery
2	large garlic cloves, chopped
1	bay leaf
1/2	teaspoon dried thyme leaves
1	package (9 ounces) frozen artichoke hearts, thawed
1	can (16 ounces) ready-cut tomatoes
1	cup low-salt chicken broth, canned or homemade (page 177)
1/4	cup dry white wine or vermouth
1/8	teaspoon crushed red pepper
10	kalamata olives, cut off pits in pieces
1/4	cup flour
	Salt and pepper
1/4	cup chopped fresh basil

1. For fresh chicken, go to step 2. If chicken is frozen, rinse 3 to 5 minutes under cold running water until flexible. Blot with paper towels and reserve on a plate.

2. In a large, heavy, ovenproof saucepan, heat 1 1/2 table-spoons of the oil over medium heat. Add onion, celery, and

garlic. Cook, stirring, 3 minutes. Add bay, thyme, and artichoke hearts. Stir to coat with oil and cook 1 minute. Stir in tomatoes, broth, wine, red pepper, and olive pieces. Bring to a boil, then reduce heat to low and simmer, partially covered, 5 minutes. Remove bay leaf.

3. Meanwhile, heat oven to 350°. Dust fresh or thawed chicken breasts with flour. Shake off excess flour. Heat remaining 1 1/2 tablespoons oil in a large, nonstick skillet. Add chicken. Sprinkle lightly with salt and pepper. Sauté 3 to 4 minutes or until golden brown. Turn and cook 1 minute more. (Chicken will not be cooked through.) Transfer, browned side up, to saucepan with sauce. Cover and bake in preheated oven until chicken is white throughout, about 20 minutes. Serve hot, sprinkled with chopped fresh basil.

Serves 4

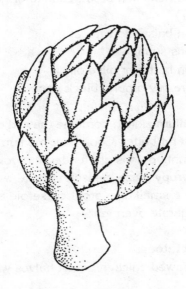

Baked Chicken Breasts with Glazed Onions and Roasted New Potatoes

Glazed onions and oven-roasted new potatoes are classic accompaniments with chicken. A garlic and herb marinade, tucked under the chicken skin, provides exceptional flavor. For this recipe, fresh chicken breasts are preferred. If chicken breasts are frozen, thaw the breasts overnight in the refrigerator. The glazed onions can be cooked ahead and reheated while the chicken and potatoes cook.

Onions:

1	package (10 ounces) frozen petite whole onions, thawed
1/2	cup low-salt chicken broth, canned or homemade (page 177)
1	tablespoon balsamic vinegar
1 1/2	tablespoons sugar
1	tablespoon butter or olive oil
	Salt and freshly ground black pepper

In a heavy, medium skillet, combine thawed onions, broth, vinegar, sugar, and butter. Cook over medium-low heat, turning frequently, until onions are tender and golden and liquid is reduced to a syrupy glaze. Season to taste with salt and pepper. Transfer to a small ovenproof casserole and set aside, or cover and refrigerate overnight.

Chicken and Potatoes:

4	fresh or thawed chicken breast halves with skins, on the bone
2	garlic cloves, pressed

1/2	tablespoon olive oil
1 1/2	teaspoons fresh lemon juice
1	teaspoon chopped fresh parsley
1/4	teaspoon dried thyme
1/4	teaspoon Worcestershire sauce
1/4	teaspoon salt
	Freshly ground black pepper
1 1/2	pounds small red new potatoes, rinsed and rubbed with olive oil

1. Preheat oven to 400°. Trim excess fat and any overhanging skin from chicken breasts, leaving most of the skin on. With a sharp knife, make a 2-inch lengthwise slit in center of each breast. Set aside. In a small bowl, combine garlic, olive oil, lemon juice, parsley, thyme, Worcestershire sauce, salt and pepper to taste. Rub the seasonings all over the breasts and into the slit part of the flesh. Arrange the breasts in a single layer in a large greased shallow oven-proof baking pan. Bake in preheated 400° oven until browned and no longer pink in thickest part of the flesh, 30 to 35 minutes.

2. At the same time, roast the potatoes in a medium baking pan until tender when pierced with tip of a sharp knife, about 35 minutes. The last 15 minutes of cooking, put the glazed onions in the oven to reheat. To serve, place one chicken breast on each of four plates, and surround evenly with potatoes and onions.

Serves 4

Roasted Chicken Breast with Basil and Sun-Dried Tomatoes

This dish is light, colorful, and quick to prepare. Offer some good crusty bread to soak up the delicious juices of the sauce.

4	fresh or frozen skinless, boneless chicken breast halves
3	tablespoons olive oil
	Salt and freshly ground black pepper
1/2	medium red bell pepper, cut into 1/2-inch cubes
4	oil-packed sun-dried tomatoes, chopped
2	garlic cloves, minced
2	green onions, including about 2 inches of green, chopped
1	tablespoon fresh lemon juice
1/4	teaspoon salt
1/4	cup chopped fresh basil, loosely packed

1. Preheat oven to 450°. Place rack in upper third of oven. For fresh chicken, go to step 2. If chicken breasts are frozen, to thaw quickly, rinse under cold running water 3 to 5 minutes or until flexible. Blot with paper towels.

2. Arrange fresh or thawed breasts on a baking sheet and brush chicken pieces lightly with some of the oil. Season with salt and pepper. Roast in preheated oven until white throughout in thickest part of the breast, 15 to 20 minutes.

3. Meanwhile, in a small skillet, heat remaining oil over medium heat. Add red pepper, sun-dried tomatoes, and garlic. Cook, stirring, until pepper is crisp-tender, about

2 minutes. Add green onions, lemon juice, salt, and pepper. Cook 30 seconds. Remove from heat and stir in basil. Place cooked chicken on individual serving plates. Spoon sauce evenly over the chicken and serve.

Serves 4

Baked Chicken with
Sautéed Cauliflower

Even cauliflower resisters like this amazing flavor combination.

4	fresh or frozen skinless, boneless chicken breast halves
	Salt and pepper
1/3	cup flour
3	tablespoons olive oil
1	tablespoon unsalted butter
1	medium cauliflower, leaves, core, and stems removed and cut into bite-size pieces
6	green onions, including 2 inches of green, chopped
1	garlic clove, minced
1/4	teaspoon crushed red pepper flakes
1/2	cup low-salt chicken broth, canned or homemade (page 177)
2	tablespoons dry sherry
1	tablespoon fresh lime or lemon juice
1/4	cup shredded Parmesan cheese
1	tablespoon chopped fresh parsley

1. For fresh chicken, go to step 2. If chicken breasts are frozen, place in sealed plastic bag and thaw in a large pan of cold water for about 35 minutes or until flexible. Blot with paper towels.

2. Trim fresh or thawed breasts of any visible fat. Sprinkle lightly with salt and pepper. Dust the breasts lightly with flour and shake off excess. In a large, nonstick skillet, heat 2 tablespoons of the olive oil over medium heat. Add

chicken and cook, until golden brown, 3 to 4 minutes. Turn and cook 3 minutes. Remove to a plate.

3. Preheat oven to 400°. In the same skillet, add remaining 1 tablespoon olive oil and the butter. Add the cauliflower, green onions, garlic, and pepper flakes. Cook, stirring frequently, until cauliflower begins to brown, about 3 minutes. Add chicken broth, sherry, and lime juice. Bring to a boil, scraping up browned bits, and cook until slightly reduced, 2 to 3 minutes. Season to taste with salt and pepper. Turn the vegetables into a 9 × 12-inch baking dish. Arrange chicken breasts in a single layer over the vegetables. Sprinkle with cheese and parsley. Bake, uncovered, in preheated oven until top is lightly browned, about 15 minutes.

Serves 4

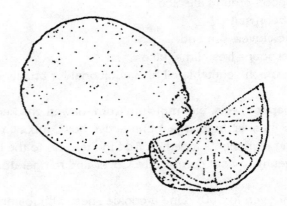

Spicy Chili-Baked Chicken Fingers

Convenient frozen chicken tenders are perfect for this dish. The spicy baked fingers can be served as a hearty appetizer or with Mexican rice and beans for a terrific combination plate. For this preparation, allow about 30 minutes to thaw frozen chicken tenders before they are tossed with the seasoning paste.

16	frozen chicken tenders (about 1 pound), thawed at room temperature, for 30 minutes
1	tablespoon pure New Mexico chili powder
1/2	teaspoon dried Mexican oregano, rubbed in palm to crumble
1/2	teaspoon ground cumin
1/4	teaspoon ground cinnamon
1/8	teaspoon ground allspice
1/4	teaspoon salt
2	garlic cloves, pressed
1 1/2	tablespoons fresh lime juice
1	tablespoon vegetable oil plus additional for brushing foil

1. With paper towels, blot moisture from thawed chicken tenders. Set aside. In a large, nonreactive bowl, mix all remaining ingredients together. Add the tenders to the bowl. Toss gently to coat completely. Cover and refrigerate for 1 hour.
2. Preheat oven to 500°. Line a cookie sheet with foil and brush foil lightly with oil. Scrape excess marinade from

chicken. Place on baking pan in a single layer. Let sit at room temperature for 10 to 15 minutes. Bake 4 to 6 minutes or until firm to the touch and no pink remains. Serve hot or at room temperature.

Serves 4

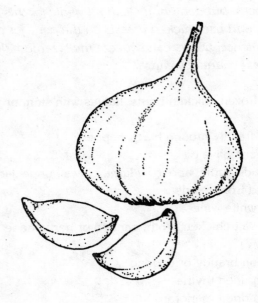

Baked Chicken with Lots of Garlic

A well-known classic dish is chicken with 40 cloves of garlic, but who's counting? Just be sure to use "lots," because the baked garlic becomes mellow and creamy. This is serious finger-lickin' fare, so supply plenty of napkins. Buy garlic heads with large cloves, but don't buy elephant garlic for this delicious version, and use chicken breasts on the bone for extra flavor and succulence. Diners can squeeze the creamy baked garlic over good country bread.

4	fresh or frozen chicken breast halves with skin, on the bone
	Salt and freshly ground black pepper
2	tablespoons olive oil
2	large heads garlic, about 30 large cloves, unpeeled and separated from heads
1/2	cup dry white wine
1/4	cup low-salt chicken broth, canned or homemade (page 177)
1	tablespoon brandy or cognac
1/2	teaspoon dried thyme
1/4	teaspoon dried marjoram
1/4	teaspoon dried oregano, crumbled
1	tablespoon chopped fresh parsley
	Sourdough or country-style bread

1. For fresh chicken, go to step 2. If breasts are frozen, thaw overnight in the refrigerator, if possible, or alternatively, place in a sealed plastic bag and thaw in a large pan of cold water for about 45 minutes or until flexible.

2. Preheat oven to 350°. Trim fresh or thawed chicken of any visible fat and excess skin, leaving part of the skin on. Sprinkle with salt and pepper. In a large, nonstick skillet, heat oil over medium heat. When oil shimmers, add the chicken, skin side down, and cook until lightly browned, 3 to 4 minutes. Turn and cook 2 minutes. (Chicken will not be cooked through.) Transfer chicken, skin side up and in a single layer, to an ovenproof earthenware or other heavy casserole.

3. To the same skillet, add the garlic cloves and cook, stirring, for 2 minutes. Add garlic to the casserole with the chicken, tucking the garlic under and between the chicken breasts.

4. Pour remaining oil out of the skillet. To the skillet, add wine, chicken broth, brandy, thyme, marjoram, and oregano. Bring to a boil over high heat, stirring to incorporate any browned bits from the skillet. Pour the liquid over the contents of the casserole. Cover tightly and bake for 40 to 45 minutes or until garlic is very tender and chicken comes easily away from the bone. Sprinkle with chopped parsley and taste for seasonings. Serve the chicken and garlic with the pan juices and thick slices of good country bread.

Serves 4

Green Chile and Olive Stuffed Chicken Breasts

Linda Hennen, of Novato, California, contributed this imaginative chicken roll recipe with the tempting flavors of green chiles, olives, and cheese. Fresh tomato salsa or a cooked enchilada sauce go well with this chicken dish. Any kind of Mexican Style beans make a good accompaniment, too.

4	fresh or frozen skinless, boneless chicken breast halves
	Salt and pepper
1	can (4 ounces) diced green chiles such as Ortega, drained
1/4	cup chopped black olives
1/4	cup packed shredded cheddar cheese
1	tablespoon finely chopped onions
1	teaspoon chili powder
2	tablespoons olive oil
1	cup crushed (with rolling pin) corn tortilla chips

1. For fresh chicken, go to step 2. If breasts are frozen, to thaw quickly, rinse under cold running water for 3 to 5 minutes or until flexible. If breasts are still partially frozen in the thickest parts, let sit at room temperature for about 20 minutes.

2. Trim fresh or thawed breasts of any visible fat. Place each breast between two sheets of plastic wrap and pound with flat side of a wooden meat mallet or a rolling pin to an even thickness of about 1/8 inch. Sprinkle with salt and pepper. Set aside.

3. Preheat oven to 375°. In a small bowl, combine chiles, olives, cheese, onions, and chili powder. Pat chicken dry with paper towels. Divide green chile mixture into four equal parts, and place one portion in the center of each breast half. Spread filling to within 1 inch of the edges. Fold in ragged edges and roll into a cylinder. Secure with toothpicks. Coat chicken rolls with olive oil, and then roll in crushed tortilla chips. Arrange chicken rolls, seam side down, on a greased baking sheet, and bake in preheated oven for 30 to 35 minutes or until breast meat is no longer pink and juices run clear when pierced with tip of a sharp knife, or interior temperature registers 160° on a kitchen thermometer. Cut crosswise on the diagonal and serve.

Serves 4

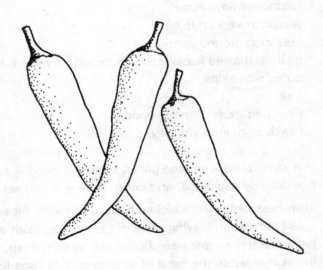

Roasted Chicken Breasts with Honey Curry Glaze

Imported Indian curry combined with lemon and honey imparts a lively flavor to oven-roasted chicken breasts. For this recipe, if using frozen chicken breasts, defrost them overnight in the refrigerator. Roasting on the bone with skins produces juicier and more succulent chicken. For an impressive entree, and to accent the Indian flavors, serve with steamed basmati rice.

1	garlic clove, pressed
3	tablespoons honey
2	tablespoons fresh lemon juice
2	teaspoons Indian curry powder
2	teaspoons soy sauce
1	teaspoon vegetable oil
1/2	teaspoon ground cumin
4	fresh or thawed frozen chicken breast halves, on the bone, with skins
	Salt
	Chopped fresh cilantro (optional)
	Peach or mango chutney

1. In a small bowl, combine garlic, honey, lemon juice, curry powder, soy sauce, oil, and cumin. Mix well and set aside.

2. Trim fresh or thawed chicken breasts of visible fat and excess flabby skin, leaving most of the skin on. With a sharp knife, cut three crosswise slits, about 1/2 inch deep, through the skin and into the meat of each breast. Season lightly with salt. Place breasts, skin side up, on a baking sheet. Brush chicken all over with marinade mixture. Preheat oven to 450°. Let chicken stand for 15 to 20 minutes.

3. Place chicken in preheated oven and roast for 15 minutes. Brush with glaze again, and continue roasting until well-browned on the surface and no pink remains in the thickest part of the meat, 10 to 12 minutes. Transfer breasts to a serving platter. Sprinkle with chopped cilantro, if desired. Spoon chutney alongside.

Serves 4

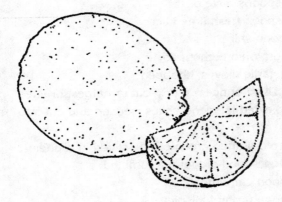

Mexican Chicken
Veracruzana

In Mexican cooking, "Veracruzana" usually refers to a fish or shrimp preparation, but the combination of ingredients is wonderful with chicken, too. Boiled new potatoes are favored with this dish.

4	fresh or frozen skinless, boneless chicken breast halves
3	tablespoons olive oil
1	tablespoon fresh lime juice
1/4	teaspoon salt
1/2	medium onion, chopped
3	large garlic cloves, chopped
1	can (14 1/2 ounces) ready-cut tomatoes, drained
3	to 4 pickled jalapeño chiles, seeded and cut into 1/8-inch strips
8	pimiento-stuffed green olives, sliced in rounds
1/2	teaspoon dried oregano, crumbled
1/4	teaspoon cinnamon
1/8	teaspoon ground allspice
2	tablespoons capers, drained
1/4	cup orange juice
1	tablespoon lemon juice
2	tablespoons chopped fresh Italian flat-leaf parsley

1. For fresh chicken, go to step 2. If breasts are frozen, to thaw quickly, rinse under cold running water for 3 to 5 minutes or until flexible. Blot with paper towels.

2. Trim fresh or thawed breasts of any visible fat. In a large, nonstick skillet, heat 2 tablespoons of the oil over medium

heat. Add chicken and cook until lightly browned on both sides, about 6 minutes total. Transfer breasts to 9 × 12-inch nonreactive, ovenproof baking dish. Drizzle with lime juice and sprinkle with salt. Set aside.

3. Preheat oven to 350°. In the same skillet, heat remaining 1 tablespoon oil over medium heat. Add onion and garlic. Cook, stirring, until softened, 3 to 4 minutes. Add tomatoes, jalapeños, olives, oregano, cinnamon, allspice, capers, and orange and lemon juices. Bring to a boil. Reduce heat to low and simmer, uncovered, 3 minutes. Spoon sauce evenly over chicken. Cover casserole loosely with aluminum foil, venting to allow steam to escape, and bake 20 to 25 minutes or until sauce is bubbling and chicken is white throughout. Sprinkle with parsley and serve.

Serves 4

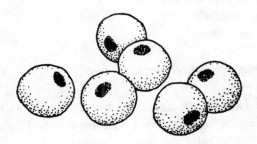

Moroccan Charmoula with Baked Chicken

Intrepid travelers and chefs, eager to taste the culinary achievements of the world, have put charmoula, Morocco's classic marinade and vinaigrette, on the map. Now everyone can experience the incredible flavors of this sauce. Serve the chicken and sauce over steamed couscous or rice. Carrots, zucchini, or green beans go well with this dish.

4	fresh or frozen skinless, boneless chicken breast halves
$1/2$	cup finely chopped fresh parsley, loosely packed
$1/2$	cup finely chopped fresh cilantro, loosely packed
2	garlic cloves, finely minced
$1/4$	cup fresh lemon juice
$1/2$	tablespoon red wine vinegar
$1 1/2$	teaspoons Hungarian paprika
$1 1/2$	teaspoons ground cumin
$1/4$	teaspoon cayenne
$1/2$	cup olive oil
	Salt and freshly ground black pepper

1. For fresh chicken, go to step 2. If breasts are frozen, place in a sealed plastic bag and thaw in a large pan of cold water for 30 to 35 minutes or until flexible.

2. Meanwhile, prepare the charmoula: In a medium bowl, combine parsley, cilantro, garlic, lemon juice, vinegar, paprika, cumin, and cayenne. Whisk in the olive oil. Season to taste with salt and pepper. (The sauce can also be made in a food processor, by pulsing the ingredients to a uniform fine texture.) Set sauce aside.

3. Preheat oven to 425°. Trim fresh or thawed breasts of any visible fat. With a sharp knife, cut three diagonal 1/2-inch deep slits on the smooth side of each breast. Put 3 teaspoons of the charmoula sauce into a small bowl. With a spoon, coat each breast with about 3/4 teaspoon of charmoula sauce. Put remaining sauce in a separate small bowl and set aside.

4. Place the breasts in a single layer, slit side up, on a foil-lined baking sheet. Bake in preheated oven for 15 to 20 minutes, depending upon the thickness of the chicken, or until juices run clear when pierced with tip of a sharp knife and meat is white throughout in the thickest part. To serve, on each of four serving plates, place one breast atop a bed of steamed couscous or rice. Spoon the remaining charmoula over the chicken, or pass remaining sauce at the table.

Serves 4

Oven-Glazed
Caribbean Chicken

Make the easy glazing sauce a day or two ahead for the flavors to meld. Rice and a tropical fruit salad or salsa goes well with the chicken.

Sauce:

1/3	cup dark brown sugar
2	tablespoons catsup
2	tablespoons dark rum
1/4	teaspoon instant coffee dissolved in 1 teaspoon water
	Juice of 1 fresh lime
1	teaspoon butter or vegetable oil
1	teaspoon minced fresh ginger
1/8	teaspoon ground allspice

In a small saucepan, combine all sauce ingredients. Bring to a boil, stirring, to melt sugar and butter, then remove from heat, cover and set aside.

Chicken:

4	fresh or frozen skinless, boneless chicken breast halves
2	large garlic cloves, pressed
1	teaspoon olive oil
1/2	teaspoon salt
1/8	teaspoon freshly ground black pepper

1. For fresh chicken, go to step 2. If chicken breasts are frozen, place in sealed plastic bag and thaw in a large pan of cold water 25 to 30 minutes or until flexible. Blot with paper towels.

2. Trim fresh or thawed chicken breasts of any visible fat. With a sharp knife, make two diagonal slits about 1/2 inch deep on the skin side of each breast. In a small bowl, combine garlic, olive oil, salt, and pepper. Rub the seasoning all over the breasts. Arrange slit side up on a rack in a shallow baking pan. Brush breast surfaces with glazing sauce. Let sit about 30 minutes.

3. Preheat oven broiler. Broil breasts for 5 minutes. Turn breasts over, coat with sauce, and broil 4 to 5 minutes. Turn breasts over again, and coat with sauce. Broil until tops are sizzling and brown, about 2 minutes. Remove from oven and serve hot.

Serves 4

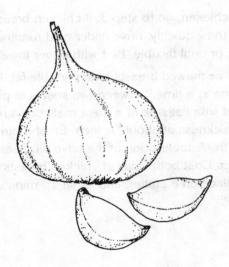

Baked Chicken Breasts with Pistachio Crust

The nut coating seals in juices and provides a pleasing texture and taste.

3/4   cup hulled pistachio nuts
1/4   cup fine bread crumbs
4   fresh or frozen skinless, boneless chicken breast halves
2 1/2 tablespoons olive oil
     Salt and pepper
     Fresh lime wedges

1. Put 3 tablespoons of the pistachios aside in a small bowl. Place remaining pistachios and bread crumbs in food processor or blender and grind to fine crumbs. Transfer to a pie plate.

2. For fresh chicken, go to step 3. If chicken breasts are frozen, to thaw quickly, rinse under cold running water 3 to 5 minutes or until flexible. Blot with paper towels.

3. Trim fresh or thawed breasts of any visible fat. Place the breasts, one at a time, between two sheets of plastic wrap and pound with flat side of a meat mallet or a rolling pin to an even thickness of about 1/2 inch. Brush both sides of breasts with 1/2 tablespoon of the olive oil. Season with salt and pepper. Coat both sides of chicken breasts with crumb mixture, place on a platter, and let sit 15 minutes. Preheat oven to 425°.

4. In a large, nonstick skillet, heat remaining oil over medium high heat. Sauté breasts for 1 minute on each side to aid in crisping the nut crust. Place on foil-lined baking sheet and bake in preheated oven 10 to 12 minutes or until white throughout but still moist. To serve, top breasts evenly with reserved pistachios and garnish with lime wedges.

Serves 4

Baked Chicken Pockets with Feta, Olives, and Almonds

Thanks to Cindy Maderos, a popular caterer from Chico, California, for sharing this delectable baked chicken breast recipe. Cindy uses it often in her catering business.

4	fresh or frozen boneless chicken breast halves, with skin
1	tablespoon olive oil
1	cup mild feta cheese
1/2	cup kalamata olives, pitted and slivered
1/4	cup finely chopped red onion
1/4	cup finely chopped toasted slivered almonds
2	tablespoons chopped oil-packed sun-dried tomatoes
1	tablespoon fresh marjoram, or 1/2 teaspoon dried
	Salt and freshly ground black pepper

1. For fresh chicken, go to step 2. If breasts are frozen, place in a sealed plastic bag and thaw in a large pan of cold water for 30 to 35 minutes or until flexible.

2. Trim fresh or thawed breasts of any visible fat and excess skin. With a sharp knife, slit each breast lengthwise, making a pocket as wide as possible without puncturing edges. Rub olive oil over outside surfaces of the breasts. Set aside.

3. Preheat oven to 375°. In a medium bowl, work together cheese, olives, onion, almonds, tomatoes, and marjoram. Fill each chicken breast pocket equally with filling. Sprinkle

skin side of breasts lightly with salt and pepper. Place in a large, heavy, shallow baking pan, skin side up, and bake 30 to 35 minues or until meat is white throughout but still juicy. Slice crosswise and serve.

Serves 4

Baked Chicken Tenders with Portobello Mushrooms

Fresh Portobello mushrooms are dark, meaty, and utterly delicious. Thanks to improved distribution, Portobellos are now widely available in the produce section of many upscale supermarkets. They range in size from about 3 inches in diameter to quite huge. Chicken breast tenders are ideal for this mouthwatering combination. Serve with rice, polenta, or pasta.

16 fresh or frozen chicken tenders (about 1 pound)
2   whole (medium) Portobello mushrooms, about 5 inches in diameter
3   tablespoons olive oil
    Salt and pepper
3   garlic cloves, minced
1/3 cup low-salt chicken broth, canned or homemade (page 177)
1   tablespoon dry white wine
2   ripe roma tomatoes, peeled, seeded, and chopped
1   tablespoon chopped fresh parsley

1. For fresh chicken, go to step 2. If chicken tenders are frozen, lay out in a single layer on a platter to thaw for about 30 minutes or until flexible.

2. Preheat oven to 450°. Remove stems from mushrooms and discard. Wipe mushrooms clean with paper towels. In a medium, nonstick skillet, heat 2 tablespoons of the olive oil over medium heat. Place whole mushrooms, top side down, in skillet. Sprinkle with salt, pepper, and garlic. Cook, turning mushrooms 2 to 3 times until juices appear, about 4

minutes. Add chicken broth and wine. Cover, reduce heat to low, and simmer, turning over once or twice, until mushrooms are tender when pierced near the center with tip of a sharp knife, 8 to 10 minutes. Remove mushrooms to a cutting surface, and let cool. When cool enough to handle, cut into thin slices, about 1/4 inch wide. Return mushrooms to skillet and reserve.

3. Meanwhile, pat chicken dry with paper towels and brush with remaining tablespoon of olive oil. Sprinkle with salt and pepper. Arrange tenders in a single layer on a large oiled baking sheet. Bake in preheated oven 6 to 8 minutes or until chicken is white throughout but still juicy. Remove from oven, and keep warm.

4. To the skillet of mushrooms, add tomatoes and bring to a boil over medium-high heat, stirring, until completely heated through, 2 to 3 minutes. Arrange chicken, mushrooms, and tomatoes with juices evenly among four serving plates. Sprinkle parsley over all, and serve.

Serves 4

Baked Chicken Breasts with Red Pepper Relish

Today's creative cooks can serve something special, like this quick, colorful dish, in a short time with the aid of a wide assortment of prepared ingredients. Add fresh corn or zucchini to complement the chicken and relish.

1	jar (7 ounces) roasted red peppers, drained and cut into 1/4-inch pieces
2	tablespoons olive oil
1	tablespoon red wine vinegar
1	tablespoon finely chopped fresh parsley
1 1/2	teaspoons drained capers
1	teaspoon soy sauce
1/8	teaspoon red chile paste
4	fresh or frozen skinless, boneless chicken breast halves
2	garlic cloves, pressed
1	teaspoon vegetable oil
1/4	teaspoon salt
	Freshly ground black pepper

1. In a medium bowl, combine red peppers, olive oil, vinegar, parsley, capers, soy sauce, and chile paste. Let stand at room temperature for 1 to 4 hours, or cover and refrigerate up to 5 days. Bring to room temperature before serving.

2. For fresh chicken, go to step 3. If breasts are frozen, place in a sealed plastic bag and thaw in a large pan of cold water for 25 to 30 minutes or until flexible.

3. Preheat oven to 425°. Trim fresh or thawed breasts of any
   visible fat. Blot with paper towels. Make a paste of garlic,
   vegetable oil, salt, and pepper. Rub all over the chicken
   breasts. Place breasts on a baking sheet, smooth side up,
   and bake in a preheated oven for 10 to 12 minutes, or until
   firm to the touch and white throughout. (If breasts are not
   completely thawed, add about 5 minutes to the baking
   time.) Serve with the red pepper relish spooned over.

Serves 4

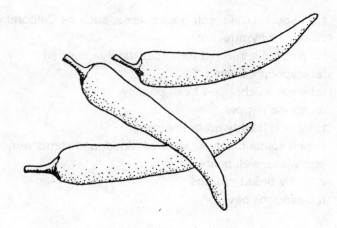

Rolled Chicken Breasts with Spinach and Goat Cheese Stuffing

These chicken rolls with colorful stuffing are something special.

4   fresh or frozen skinless, boneless chicken breast halves
      Salt
4   tablespoons mild, soft goat cheese, such as California chèvre or Montrachet
4   oil-packed sun-dried tomatoes, finely chopped
1   tablespoon currants
1   tablespoon chopped fresh parsley
1/4 teaspoon pepper
1/8 teaspoon freshly grated nutmeg
1   bunch spinach leaves, washed, dried, and stems removed
1   egg white, well beaten
1/2 cup dry bread crumbs
3   tablespoons olive oil

1. For fresh chicken, go to step 2. If chicken breasts are frozen, place in sealed plastic bag and thaw in a large pan of cold water 30 to 35 minutes or until flexible. Blot with paper towels.

2. Trim fresh or thawed breasts of any visible fat. Place breasts between two sheets of plastic wrap and pound with flat side of a meat mallet or a rolling pin to about 1/8-inch thickness. Sprinkle lightly with salt. Set aside.

3. In a small bowl, work together the goat cheese, sun-dried tomatoes, currants, parsley, pepper, and nutmeg. Lay out

the flattened chicken breasts. Using fingers, spread breasts equally with the goat cheese mixture to within $1/2$ inch of edges. Cover each with 2 layers of spinach leaves. (Store remaining leaves for salad or another use.) Fold in the ragged edges to meet in the center, and roll into cylinders. Secure with toothpicks. Put egg white in a shallow bowl and put bread crumbs on a plate. Brush rolled breasts all over with egg white, and roll in crumbs. Put on a plate and re-frigerate for 20 minutes.

4. Preheat oven to 400°. Heat oil in a large, nonstick skillet over medium-high heat and brown rolls, turning, for 3 to 4 minutes. Place seam side down on a foil-lined baking sheet and bake in preheated oven 15 to 20 minutes or until crisp on the outside and white throughout. To serve, cut each roll, on an angle, in half. Arrange on serving plates to show the filling.

Serves 4

Broiled Chicken with Romesco Sauce

Spain's zesty romesco sauce tastes good with lots of things, especially simple broiled chicken, as in this recipe. The sauce is served at room temperature and can be made ahead. Thick slices of roasted red peppers and tender, creamy white beans are good accompaniments.

Sauce:

1   large ripe tomato
2   garlic cloves, with skins on
12   whole almonds with skins
1   dried ancho chile, seeded and soaked 30 minutes in hot water
1/2   cup olive oil
2   slices (1/4 inch thick) French bread, toasted and roughly torn
2   tablespoons red wine vinegar
1   tablespoon roughly chopped fresh parsley
1/4   teaspoon crushed red pepper flakes
      Salt and freshly ground black pepper

Under a broiler, or directly over gas flame, roast the tomato until charred. Peel, quarter, and put into blender jar. In a dry, hot skillet, toast garlic cloves until aromatic and skins are flecked with brown. Peel and drop into blender jar. In same skillet, toast almonds, stirring, until aromatic. Add to blender jar, along with remaining ingredients. Puree until nearly smooth. Sauce will have some texture. Transfer to a serving bowl, and serve at room temperature. Sauce keeps, refrigerated, up to 5 days.

Chicken:

4   fresh or frozen skinless, boneless chicken breast halves
1   teaspoon dry sherry
1   teaspoon olive oil
$1/2$ teaspoon salt
$1/4$ teaspoon white pepper
$1/4$ teaspoon dried oregano
$1/4$ teaspoon dried rosemary

1. For fresh chicken, go to step 2. If chicken breasts are frozen, place in a sealed plastic bag and thaw in a pan of cold water about 30 to 35 minutes or until flexible. Blot with paper towels.

2. Trim fresh or frozen breasts of any visible fat, then one at a time, place breasts between two sheets of plastic wrap and pound with flat side of a meat mallet or a rolling pin to an even thickness of $1/2$ inch. Set aside on a platter. In a small bowl, combine sherry, olive oil, salt, pepper, oregano, and rosemary. Rub the seasoning mixture all over the breasts and let sit for about 15 minutes.

3. Preheat oven broiler and place rack in top of oven. Place breasts in one layer on a foil-lined baking sheet. Broil about 4 minutes, turn, and broil another 3 to 4 minutes or until white throughout. Cut breasts crosswise, into thin slices, and arrange, overlapping, on a serving platter. Spoon a little romesco sauce over the chicken. Pass remaining sauce at the table.

Serves 4

Roasted Chicken Breast with Savory Stuffing

For best flavor and jucier meat, purchase fresh whole chicken breasts on the bone with the skin. If using frozen chicken, thaw the whole breasts overnight in the refrigerator. This is a special-occasion dish and worth the preparation time. Serve with baked yams or sweet potatoes and a seasonal fresh vegetable.

4   cups finely torn bits of day-old sweet French bread
2   tablespoons olive oil plus additional for lightly brushing foil
1   small onion, finely chopped
2   garlic cloves, finely chopped
1/2 teaspoon dried thyme leaves
8   kalamata olives, pitted and chopped
4   oil-packed sun-dried tomatoes, finely diced
3   to 4 grinds fresh black pepper
2/3 cup low-salt chicken broth, canned or homemade (page 177)
1   tablespoon dry sherry or vermouth
2   whole fresh chicken breasts, on the bone, with skins
     Salt

1. Place bread bits in a medium bowl. Set aside. In a medium skillet, heat oil over medium heat. Add onion and garlic and cook, stirring until softened, 3 to 4 minutes. Transfer to bowl with bread. Add thyme, olives, sun-dried tomatoes, and pepper. Toss to combine. Add broth and sherry, and mix well until bread is moistened.

2. Preheat oven to 375°. Place rack in upper third of the oven. Line a baking sheet with heavy-duty aluminum foil. Fold edges up all around and brush foil lightly with olive oil. With your hands, take half the stuffing mixture and form into a rounded loaf approximately the size and shape of the breasts. Place on greased foil. Repeat with remaining half of stuffing. Allow about 3 inches of space between the stuffing mounds. Sprinkle chicken breasts all over with salt, rubbing a little under the skin. Lay one breast on each mound of stuffing. Fold edges of the foil close to the chicken breasts, but do not cover. Roast 40 to 45 minutes or until golden brown and internal temperature of chicken reads 160° on meat thermometer. Remove from oven. Carefully remove each breast half from the bones, and serve with a portion of the stuffing.

Serves 4

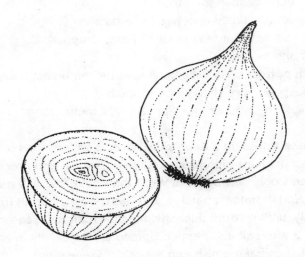

Baked Chicken with Sofrito and Asparagus

Sofrito is a basic sauce of finely chopped vegetables from the Catalan region of Spain. The sauce often contains bits of ham or sausage. In this dish, chicken breasts are quickly browned, then placed on the sofrito and baked. Fresh-cooked asparagus tips are added just before serving. An earthenware casserole is perfect for this dish.

4	tablespoons olive oil
1	medium onion, finely chopped
3	garlic cloves, finely chopped
1	green bell pepper, seeded and finely chopped
4	ripe medium tomatoes, peeled, seeded, and chopped, or 1 1/2 cups canned tomatoes
2	tablespoons finely chopped fresh parsley
1/2	cup (about 2 ounces) smoked ham, chopped
	Salt and pepper
4	fresh or frozen skinless, boneless chicken breast halves
2	tablespoons dry sherry or vermouth
12	cooked fresh asparagus tips, about 4 inches long

1. To make sofrito, in a large skillet heat 2 tablespoons of the oil over medium-high heat. Add onion, garlic, and green pepper. Cook, stirring, until vegetables soften, 4 to 5 minutes. Add tomatoes, parsley, and ham. Cook, stirring frequently, until mixture thickens, about 4 minutes. Season to taste with salt and pepper. Spread sofrito evenly in an 8 × 11-inch baking dish and set aside. Preheat oven to 350°.

2. For fresh chicken, go to step 3. If chicken breasts are frozen, to thaw quickly, rinse under running water 3 to 5 minutes or until flexible. Blot with paper towels.

3. Trim fresh or thawed breasts of any visible fat. Sprinkle lightly with salt and pepper. In a large, nonstick skillet, heat remaining 2 tablespoons of oil over medium-high heat. Add chicken and sauté on both sides until lightly browned, about 6 minutes total. (Chicken will not be cooked through.) Place chicken on the sofrito, tucking the chicken into the mixture.

   Add sherry to the hot skillet. Bring to a boil stirring and scraping pan bottom for 30 to 40 seconds to incorporate brown bits. Pour over the chicken in the baking dish. Cover with foil and bake in preheated oven for 25 to 30 minutes or until sauce is bubbling and chicken is white throughout. Arrange the cooked asparagus tips between the pieces of chicken, and serve from the casserole.

Serves 4

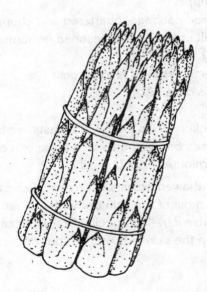

Baked Stuffed Chicken on Cabbage Bed

This is a rustic country dish well-suited to cold weather dining. Baked winter squash or mashed potatoes are a welcome addition to the plate.

4	fresh or frozen boneless chicken breast halves with skins
1	link (about 4 ounces) Italian pork sausage (hot or mild)
2	tablespoons chopped red bell pepper
1	green onion, chopped
1/4	teaspoon ground cinnamon
3/4	cup fresh bread crumbs, loosely packed
1/4	cup raisins
2	tablespoons dry white wine or chicken broth
1	tablespoon chopped, slivered almonds
	Salt and pepper
1	medium head cabbage, quartered and chopped
1/2	cup low-salt chicken broth, canned or homemade (page 177)
3/4	cup ready-cut salsa-style tomatoes
2	tablespoons olive oil

1. For fresh chicken, go to step 2. If breasts are frozen, place in sealed plastic bag and thaw in a large pan of cold water for 35 to 40 minutes or until flexible.

2. Trim fresh or thawed breasts of any visible fat and excess skin, leaving most of the skin on. With a small sharp knife, cut a lengthwise 2 1/2-inch pocket in the thickest part of the flesh, between the skin side and bottom of the breasts,

being careful not to cut all the way through. Put breasts on a plate and set aside.

3. Remove casing from the sausage. Heat a medium, nonstick skillet over medium heat. Pinch the sausage into pieces and add to the skillet, breaking up into bits as it cooks, until sausage begins to brown. Add red pepper, green onion, and cinnamon. Cook, stirring for 1 minute. Remove skillet from heat and stir in bread crumbs, raisins, wine, and almonds. Set aside to cool for about 10 minutes.

4. Lay chicken breasts, skin side down, on a working surface, and place about 2 tablespoons of the cooled stuffing into the pocket of each breast. Press cut edges together to enclose stuffing. Season breasts lightly with salt and pepper. Set aside.

5. Preheat oven to 375°. Put cabbage into a 3-quart ovenproof casserole and spread flat. Pour chicken broth and tomatoes over the cabbage. Cover the casserole and place in oven to begin cooking. In a large nonstick skillet, heat olive oil over medium-high heat. Add chicken, skin side down, and cook, turning once, to lightly brown both sides, 3 to 4 minutes. (Chicken will not be cooked through.) Arrange breasts, skin sides up, on top of cabbage in casserole. Cover the casserole, and bake in preheated oven for 35 to 40 minutes or until cabbage is tender and chicken juices run clear when pierced with tip of a sharp knife. Serve hot.

Serves 4

Tandoori Chicken

Tandoori chicken is one of India's most liked and well-known dishes. It is traditionally roasted in a special clay oven, but baking in a regular home oven gives very good results. Chicken breasts must be marinated overnight, so plan ahead. Aromatic basmati rice is wonderful with the chicken. Look for it in specialty markets or health food stores. Fresh tomato and cucumber salad also goes well with this dish.

4	fresh or frozen skinless, boneless chicken breast halves
1/2	teaspoon salt
1/2	medium onion, chopped
1	teaspoon finely chopped fresh ginger
3	garlic cloves, chopped
1	teaspoon Indian curry powder
1/2	teaspoon paprika
1/4	teaspoon cayenne
1/2	cup plain yogurt, lowfat or regular
2	tablespoons fresh lemon juice
1	teaspoon vegetable oil
	Freshly ground black pepper
	Fresh mint
	Prepared chutney

1. For fresh chicken, go to step 2. If breasts are frozen, to thaw quickly, rinse under cold running water 3 to 5 minutes or until flexible. Blot with paper towels.

2. Cut three diagonal gashes 1/2 inch deep in each fresh or thawed chicken breast. Rub with salt. Place breasts in a sealed plastic bag. Set aside.

3. In food processor, or blender, process until smooth the onion, ginger, garlic, curry powder, paprika, cayenne, yogurt, and lemon juice. Pour marinade into plastic bag with the chicken. Seal bag, and turn several times to coat chicken well. Refrigerate overnight, turning bag over once or twice to distribute marinade evenly.

4. Preheat oven to 500°. Scrape most of the marinade off chicken breasts and arrange on a foil-lined baking sheet. With a brush, dab a little oil on the breasts. Sprinkle breast lightly with freshly ground pepper. Bake about 12 minutes or until golden on the surface and white throughout. Serve hot, garnished with mint and chutney.

Serves 4

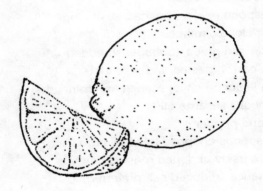

Broiled Teriyaki Chicken on Braised Cabbage with Green Onions and Ginger

A simple teriyaki marinade makes chicken taste terrific, and it goes especially well with the Asian flavors of the braised cabbage.

4	fresh or frozen skinless, boneless chicken breast halves
1/4	cup bottled teriyaki marinade
3	tablespoons vegetable oil
1/8	teaspoon freshly ground black pepper
4	green onions, sliced
1	tablespoon peeled, minced fresh ginger
2	garlic cloves, minced
1	small head green cabbage, shredded
1	large carrot, peeled and shredded
1	fresh jalapeño chile, seeded and minced
2	teaspoons sesame oil
	Salt and pepper
2	tablespoons chopped fresh cilantro
1/4	cup coarsely chopped roasted peanuts
	Soy sauce (reduced salt preferred)

1. For fresh chicken, go to step 2. If chicken breasts are frozen, place in sealed plastic bag and thaw in a large pan of cold water for about 35 minutes or until flexible. Blot with paper towels.

2. Trim fresh or thawed chicken breasts of any visible fat. Place breasts between two sheets of plastic wrap and pound with flat side of a meat mallet or a rolling pin to an

even thickness of $1/4$ inch. Place on a platter and pour on teriyaki marinade and 1 tablespoon of the vegetable oil. Turn several times to coat with marinade. Cover and refrigerate 2 to 6 hours.

3. Shortly before serving, preheat oven broiler and place rack in top position. Put chicken breasts on a foil-lined baking sheet and broil about 5 minutes, then turn and broil 3 to 4 minutes or until white throughout. Remove from oven and reserve.

4. In a large, deep skillet, heat remaining 2 tablespoons oil over medium heat. Add green onions, ginger, and garlic. Cook, stirring, for 1 minute. Add cabbage, carrot, jalapeño, sesame oil, and 3 tablespoons water. Season to taste with salt and pepper. Cook, stirring frequently, 4 to 5 minutes or until cabbage is wilted. Place reserved broiled chicken on top of the cabbage. Cover and cook over low heat for 5 minutes. To serve, divide cabbage equally among four serving plates. Slice each breast crosswise and arrange on top of the cabbage. Sprinkle with chopped cilantro and peanuts. Pass a small bowl of soy sauce at the table.

Serves 4

Roasted Chicken Breasts
with Tarragon

Serve this no-fuss oven-roasted chicken with a selection of seasonal vegetables for a contemporary and healthy entree. Fresh tarragon, garlic, and lemon coat the meat under the skin to season the chicken.

4	fresh or frozen chicken breast halves, with skins
2	garlic cloves, pressed
2	tablespoons chopped fresh tarragon
1	tablespoon fresh lemon juice
2	teaspoons soft butter
1/4	teaspoon salt
1/8	teaspoon pepper
	Olive oil

1. For fresh chicken, go to step 2. If chicken breasts are frozen, place in sealed plastic bag and thaw in a large pan of cold water for about 45 minutes or until flexible. Blot with paper towels.

2. Preheat oven to 400° and move rack to upper third of oven. Trim fresh or thawed breasts of excess fat, leaving skins intact. In a small bowl, mix together garlic, tarragon, lemon juice, butter, salt, and pepper. Lift the skin of the breasts and slide fingers between skin and flesh to make a pocket. Stuff the seasoning mixture equally under the skin on each breast. Rub remaining seasoning all over skin surfaces. Brush skins lightly with olive oil. Place breasts on a baking sheet and roast in upper third of preheated oven for 30 to 35 minutes or until meat is white throughout but still juicy.

Serves 4

4

Savory One Dish Combinations

Casseroles and stews speak of home and cozy times. Nothing seems quite so welcoming, satisfying, or comforting than a hearty bowl of steaming stew or a bubbling casserole hot from the oven. They are economical, easy to make, and can usually be made ahead and reheated. Even delicate chicken breasts stand up to reheating in these great one-dish main courses. Stews and casseroles are terrific for simple and casual entertaining. Casseroles come straight from the oven to the table in their own cooking vessel, and stews can be served in handsome tureens or attractive heavy country bowls.

For cooking stews, use heavy saucepans and enameled cast-iron pots with tight-fitting lids to hold in moisture while the stews simmer. Heavy stew pots also help prevent sticking and allow even heat distribution. There are many choices of casseroles. They can be round, oval, square, or rectangular. They can be deep or shallow. They can be made of ovenproof glass, ceramic, or glazed earthenware. When it's necessary to cover casseroles without lids, aluminum foil serves well.

Chicken breasts require less cooking time than other meats, so when preparing a casserole or stew that features chicken breasts, you will often brown or poach the breasts at the beginning, remove them from the pan until other ingredients reach a certain point, then return the breasts for the final cooking. This method prevents overcooking and keeps the meat tender. Stews and casseroles also derive much of their flavor from stocks and broths. Since chicken breasts are so mild in flavor, it's important to use full-flavored cooking liquids. For those who wish to make their own stock, there is a recipe for homemade chicken stock at the beginning of this chapter. Good-quality low-sodium and no-fat canned chicken broth is used a great deal, too. There are also improved instant bouillons on the market, which can perk up flavor; most are high in sodium, so use sparingly in conjunction with other broths.

This chapter contains a mouth-watering selection of scrumptious stews and time-honored casseroles, which make ideal complete meals. Just add a favorite bread and perhaps a green salad and a delectable sweet to round out a relaxed and friendly meal. Turn to the recipes in this chapter for homey dishes to please all your family and guests.

Homemade Chicken Stock

Throughout this book, chicken stock or canned low-salt broth is an essential part of most recipes. They are interchangeable; however, homemade stock is richer, more flavorful, and less salty than canned broths. For cooks who wish to make their own, this basic stock requires several hours of simmering, but it is easy to assemble. Freeze the finished stock in convenient 1-pint freezer containers. It keeps frozen for up to 6 months.

4	pounds chicken parts, wings, backs, and necks
2	medium onions, chopped
2	medium carrots, chopped
1	large rib celery, sliced crosswise
3	to 4 parsley sprigs
2	garlic cloves, quartered
2	bay leaves

Rinse chicken parts and put them into a large stockpot. Cover with 4 quarts cold water. Bring to a boil over medium-high heat, then reduce heat to low, and skim surface as needed. Simmer, partially covered, for 30 minutes. Add remaining ingredients and simmer, uncovered, 3 to 4 hours. With a slotted spoon, remove solids and discard. Pour stock through a fine-mesh strainer into a large glass or stainless steel container. Cool, then refrigerate until cold. Remove fat layer from the top. Pour into 1-pint freezer containers and freeze.

Makes about 3 quarts

Chicken and Pearl Barley Stew

In ancient times, barley provided sustenance and nutrition to much of the population when there was very little else available, but don't wait for hard times to dine on this remarkable grain. Although packaged pearl barley is processed, it still delivers a healthy amount of protein and minerals. Combined with morsels of chicken and a variety of vegetables, it makes a memorable and comforting stew.

1/2   cup uncooked pearl barley
4   fresh or frozen skinless, boneless chicken breast halves
2   tablespoons olive oil
1   tablespoon unsalted butter
1   medium onion, chopped
3   large garlic cloves, chopped
6   medium Crimini (brown) mushrooms, coarsely chopped
2   medium carrots, peeled and cut into 1/4-inch pieces
1   medium parsnip, peeled and chopped (remove and discard tough center core)
1   large rib celery, chopped
2   cups low-salt chicken broth, canned or homemade (page 177)
1   cup canned beef broth
1   cup canned stewed tomatoes, chopped, undrained
1/2   cup dry white wine
1   tablespoon Hungarian paprika
2   bay leaves
1   teaspoon dried oregano, crumbled
1   teaspoon dried thyme
1/8   teaspoon freshly grated nutmeg
      Salt and freshly ground black pepper

1. In a medium pan, soak the barley in 1 cup of water for 5 to 6 hours or overnight in the refrigerator. For fresh chicken, go to step 2. If chicken breasts are frozen, thaw overnight in the refrigerator or thaw in a sealed plastic bag for 30 to 35 minutes or until flexible.

2. Trim fresh or thawed chicken of any visible fat. Cut into bite-size pieces. Set aside. In a large, heavy Dutch oven or saucepan, heat oil and butter over medium heat. Add onion and garlic. Cook, stirring, until softened, 3 to 4 minutes. Add the chicken pieces and cook, stirring frequently, until no longer pink, 3 to 4 minutes. Add the remaining ingredients, except the barley, salt, and pepper. Cover and cook, stirring frequently, until the vegetables are barely tender, 10 to 12 minutes. Drain the water from the barley and stir barley into the stew. Cover and cook the stew until thickened and the barley is tender, about 15 minutes. Season to taste with salt and pepper. If stew becomes too thick, add additional broth or stewed tomatoes, 1/4 cup at a time, to reach desired consistency. Serve hot, in shallow soup plates.

Serves 4 to 6

Chunky Chicken, Spinach, and Mushroom Casserole

Some folks get a craving for creamy spinach. This lowfat version with plenty of tender chicken is nutritious and satisfying.

2	packages (10 ounces each) frozen chopped spinach
3	fresh or frozen skinless, boneless chicken breast halves
	Salt and pepper
2 1/2	tablespoons olive oil
1/2	medium onion, finely chopped
2	garlic cloves, finely chopped
1 1/2	tablespoons flour
3/4	cup low-salt chicken broth, canned or homemade (page 177)
3/4	cup lowfat or whole milk
4	medium mushrooms, halved and thinly sliced
1/4	cup freshly grated best-quality Parmesan cheese

1. Cook the frozen spinach according to package directions. Drain and squeeze out as much liquid as possible. Place chopped spinach in a large, nonreactive bowl. Set aside.

2. For fresh chicken, go to step 3. If breasts are frozen, to thaw quickly, rinse under cold running water for 3 to 5 minutes or until flexible.

3. Preheat oven to 350°. Butter a shallow 2-quart ovenproof casserole. Trim fresh or thawed breasts of any visible fat. Cut into 1/2-inch pieces. Pat dry with paper towels. Sprinkle with salt and pepper. In a large, nonstick skillet, heat 1 1/2 tablespoons of the oil over medium heat and cook chicken pieces, stirring, until no longer pink, 2 to 3 minutes. Using

slotted spoon, transfer chicken to the bowl with the spinach.

4. In the same skillet, add remaining 1 tablespoon of oil and cook onion and garlic until softened, 3 to 4 minutes. Adjust heat to prevent burning. Stir in the flour and cook 1 minute. Add broth and milk, stirring. Bring to a boil and cook until smooth and slightly thickened, 2 to 3 minutes. Remove skillet from heat and season to taste with salt and pepper.

5. Pour sauce over chicken pieces and spinach. Add mushrooms and stir to combine. Turn contents into the buttered casserole. Sprinkle with Parmesan cheese and bake in preheated oven 25 to 30 minutes or until bubbly and top is lightly browned. If top does not brown, run under broiler for 2 to 3 minutes. Serve hot.

Serves 4

Country Captain

East Indian spices flavor this old-fashioned American stew dish, popular in the south. The story goes that it was introduced by a certain sea captain during colonial times. Resurrected, revised, and lightened, it makes a marvelous meal.

4	fresh or frozen skinless, boneless chicken breast halves
1/4	teaspoon salt
1/8	teaspoon freshly ground black pepper
1 1/2	tablespoons olive oil
2	medium carrots, peeled and sliced
1	medium onion, chopped
1	medium green bell pepper, seeded and cut into 1/2-inch pieces
2	large garlic cloves, chopped
2	teaspoons Indian curry powder
1	can (14 1/2 ounces) diced or ready-cut tomatoes with juices
3/4	cup low-salt chicken broth, canned or homemade (page 177)
3	tablespoons dried currants
1/3	cup slivered blanched almonds, toasted
	Mango chutney

1. For fresh chicken, go to step 2. If chicken breasts are frozen, rinse under cold running water 3 to 5 minutes or until flexible. Blot with paper towels.

2. Cut fresh or thawed breasts into 3 or 4 equal pieces. Season chicken pieces with salt and pepper. In a large, nonstick skillet, heat oil over medium heat. Cook chicken

pieces until lightly browned on both sides, about 4 minutes total. Remove to a side dish.

3. To the skillet, add carrots, onion, green pepper, and garlic. Cook over medium heat, stirring, about 2 minutes. Stir in curry powder and combine well. Add tomatoes, chicken broth, currants, and reserved chicken. Bring to a boil, then reduce heat to low, cover, and simmer slowly about 20 minutes or until vegetables are tender. Serve hot, sprinkled with almonds. Spoon chutney alongside.

Serves 4

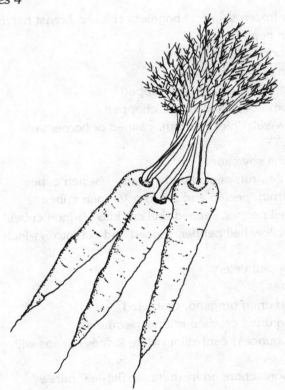

Mediterranean Chicken Stew with White Beans

Since chicken breasts require only a short time to cook, a beautiful lowfat stew can be made quickly. This one has plenty of nutritious vegetables, creamy cannellini beans, and tender chicken pieces. In blustery weather, this dish is especially enjoyed with crusty bread and a glass of wine.

3	fresh or frozen skinless, boneless chicken breast halves
	Salt and pepper
3	tablespoons olive oil
1/2	medium onion, chopped
3	large garlic cloves, finely chopped
3	roma tomatoes, peeled and chopped
2	cups low-salt chicken broth, canned or homemade (page 177)
2	teaspoons soy sauce
1	medium carrot, peeled and cut into 1/3-inch cubes
1	small turnip, peeled and cut into 1/3-inch cubes
1/2	green bell pepper, seeded and cut into 1/3-inch cubes
1/2	red or yellow bell pepper, seeded and cut into 1/3-inch cubes
1/2	cup chopped celery
2	bay leaves
1	teaspoon dried oregano, crumbled
1/8	teaspoon dried crushed red pepper flakes
1	can (15 ounces) cannellini (white kidney) beans with juices
2	tablespoons chopped fresh Italian flat-leaf parsley
2	tablespoons fresh lemon juice
	Grated Parmesan cheese (optional)

1. For fresh chicken, go to step 2. If chicken breasts are frozen, place in sealed plastic bag and thaw in a large pan of cold water about 35 minutes or until flexible. Blot with paper towels.

2. Trim fresh or thawed breasts of any visible fat, and cut into 1-inch pieces. Sprinkle lightly with salt and pepper. In a heavy, large saucepan, heat oil over medium heat until it shimmers. Cook chicken pieces, in two batches, tossing until no longer pink, 3 to 4 minutes per batch. Using a slotted spoon, transfer breast pieces to a bowl. Set aside.

3. In the same saucepan, cook onion and garlic 3 minutes, scraping browned bits from pan bottom. Add tomatoes and cook until juices evaporate and mixture is nearly dry. Add broth, soy sauce, carrot, turnip, bell peppers, celery, bay, oregano, and red pepper flakes. Bring to a boil, then reduce heat to medium-low and cook, partially covered, until vegetables are barely tender, 5 to 6 minutes. Add the beans, parsley, chicken pieces, and lemon juice. Stir to combine. Bring to a boil, reduce heat to medium-low, cover, and simmer 5 minutes. Season to taste with salt and pepper. Serve with a sprinkling of grated Parmesan cheese, if desired.

Serves 4

Chicken Casserole with Mushrooms and Noodles

This comforting casserole is fit for family or guests.

4	fresh or frozen skinless, boneless chicken breast halves
1	bag (12 ounces) dried egg noodles
	Salt and pepper
2	tablespoons flour
1	tablespoon unsalted butter
1	tablespoon vegetable oil
1/2	pound medium mushrooms, sliced (2 cups)
2	garlic cloves, minced
1	can (2 ounces) pimiento strips
1	tablespoon parsley
1	cup low-salt chicken broth, canned or homemade (page 177)
1	cup heavy cream
3/4	cup (3 ounces) shredded Swiss cheese

1. For fresh chicken breasts, go to step 2. If chicken breasts are frozen, place in sealed plastic bag and thaw in a large pan of cold water about 35 minutes or until flexible. Blot with paper towels.

2. Trim fresh or thawed breasts of any visible fat, cut each breast into 3 equal pieces and set aside.

3. In a large pot of boiling salted water, cook egg noodles until done, according to package instructions. Drain and toss noodles with a few drops of oil. Place in a buttered oven-proof casserole. Set aside.

4. Preheat oven to 350°. Sprinkle chicken pieces lightly with salt and pepper. Dust with flour. In a large, nonstick skillet, heat butter and oil over medium heat and sauté chicken, turning, until golden, 6 to 8 minutes total. Arrange chicken evenly over the noodles. In the same skillet, cook mushrooms and garlic, stirring, until mushrooms appear juicy, about 3 minutes. Stir in pimiento strips, parsley, broth, and cream. Bring to a boil, remove from heat, and taste sauce for seasoning. Add salt and pepper, if needed. Pour the sauce evenly over chicken and noodles, pressing gently with back of spoon to push noodles into the sauce. Sprinkle top with cheese. Bake in preheated oven until bubbling and cheese is melted, about 25 minutes. Serve from the casserole.

Serves 4 to 6

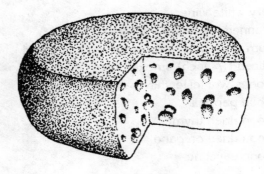

New Orleans
Smothered Chicken

For a taste of the new New Orleans cooking, try this calorie-controlled entree. For a perfect companion, serve the chicken stew with soft creamy grits.

4   fresh or frozen skinless, boneless chicken breast halves
     Salt and pepper
3   tablespoons vegetable oil
1   large onion, chopped
3   garlic cloves, chopped
1/2 green bell pepper, seeded and chopped
1   large rib celery, chopped
1   tablespoon flour
1/2 cup low-salt chicken broth, canned or homemade
     (page 177)
1/4 cup dry white wine
3/4 cup canned ready-cut tomatoes
12   medium fresh mushrooms, halved and sliced
1/2 cup diced (1/4 inch) smoked ham
1 1/2 teaspoons Worcestershire sauce
1   teaspoon paprika
1/2 teaspoon dried thyme
1/2 teaspoon dried oregano
1/4 teaspoon cayenne

1. For fresh chicken, go to step 2. If chicken breasts are
   frozen, place in a sealed plastic bag and thaw in a large pan
   of cold water for 25 to 30 minutes or until flexible. Blot with
   paper towels.

2. Preheat oven to 350°. Trim fresh or thawed breasts of any visible fat. Sprinkle breasts lightly with salt and pepper. In a heavy, large, deep skillet, heat 2 tablespoons of the oil over medium-high heat. Add chicken and cook, turning, until lightly browned on both sides, about 6 minutes total. (Chicken will not be cooked through.) Transfer chicken to a 2-quart ovenproof casserole. Set aside.

3. To the same skillet, add remaining 1 tablespoon oil, onion, garlic, green pepper, and celery. Cook, stirring, until vegetables are softened, 4 to 5 minutes. Stir in flour and cook 1 minute. All at once, add broth, wine, and tomatoes. Cook, stirring rapidly, until mixture boils and thickens. Add remaining ingredients. Bring to a boil. Pour contents over chicken. Cover the casserole loosely with foil and bake in preheated oven 30 to 35 minutes or until bubbling throughout.

Serves 4

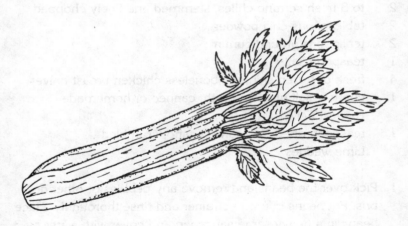

No-Fat Black Jack Chicken Chili

Amazing, but true. This incendiary black bean and chicken chili has no added fat, yet it's completely satisfying as a full meal. This chili is adapted from a recipe given to me by my friend, Kathy Hanley. Serve with tortillas or crusty bread.

16	ounces dried black beans
1	can (14 1/2 ounces) ready-cut tomatoes, with juice
1	can (8 ounces) tomato sauce
1	large red onion, finely chopped
1	bunch cilantro, washed, heavy stems removed and chopped
6	large garlic cloves, chopped
2	to 3 fresh serrano chiles, stemmed and finely chopped
2	tablespoons chili powder
2	teaspoons ground cumin
1	teaspoon salt
4	fresh or frozen skinless, boneless chicken breast halves
1	cup low-salt chicken broth, canned or homemade (page 177)
1	teaspoon dried Mexican oregano, crumbled
	Lime wedges

1. Pick over the beans and remove any pebbles or other debris. Put beans in a wire strainer and rinse thoroughly. Place beans in a heavy, large saucepan and cover with water by 3 inches. Bring to a boil, uncovered, over medium-high heat. Boil 2 minutes. Cover and turn off heat. Let beans soak 1 hour, then cook, covered, over low heat for 1 hour or until tender. Add tomatoes, tomato sauce, onion, cilantro, garlic,

serranos, chili powder, cumin, and salt. Bring to a boil, over medium-high heat, stirring frequently, then reduce heat to low, cover, and simmer for 1 hour.

2. Meanwhile, prepare chicken. If chicken is fresh, go to step 3. If breasts are frozen, place in a sealed plastic bag and thaw in a large pan of cold water for 25 to 30 minutes or until flexible.

3. Trim fresh or thawed chicken of any visible fat and cut into bite-size pieces. In a medium skillet, heat broth over medium heat until it begins to simmer. Add chicken pieces and oregano. Reduce heat to medium-low, cover, and simmer until chicken is no longer pink, 3 to 4 minutes. Turn off heat and leave chicken in the broth. 30 minutes before serving, add chicken and the broth to the chili. Simmer chili 30 minutes, and serve hot. Serve lime wedges at the table to squeeze juice over the chile.

Serves 6

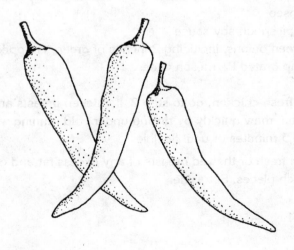

Old-Fashioned Chicken and Rice Casserole

An updated version of a popular '50s-style casserole contains less fat and sodium. It's still delicious and it's healthier, too.

4	fresh or frozen skinless, boneless chicken breast halves
1/2	cup long-grain rice
2	tablespoons vegetable oil
1/2	cup chopped celery
6	medium fresh mushrooms, sliced
1/4	teaspoon salt
1/8	teaspoon pepper
1 1/2	tablespoons flour
1	cup low-salt chicken broth, canned or homemade (page 177)
3/4	cup milk
1/2	cup (5 ounce can) sliced water chestnuts, drained and rinsed
1	tablespoon soy sauce
4	green onions, including 2 inches of green, chopped
1/4	cup grated Parmesan cheese

1. For fresh chicken, go to step 2. If chicken breasts are frozen, thaw quickly by rinsing under cold running water for 3 to 5 minutes or until flexible.

2. Trim fresh or thawed breasts of any excess fat and cut into 1-inch pieces. Set aside.

3. In a medium saucepan, cook rice in 1 cup boiling, salted water, uncovered for 5 minutes. Drain and reserve. (Rice will not be tender.)

4. Preheat oven to 350°. In a large skillet, heat oil over medium heat. Cook celery, stirring, until crisp-tender, about 2 minutes. Add chicken pieces and mushrooms. Cook, stirring, until chicken is no longer pink, 2 to 3 minutes. Add salt, pepper, and flour. Stir well to combine. Add broth and milk all at once. Bring to a boil, stirring, and cook until slightly thickened. Remove pan from heat. Add water chestnuts, soy sauce, green onions, and rice.

5. Transfer to a 2-quart baking dish. Sprinkle cheese evenly over chicken and rice. Bake in preheated oven for 25 to 30 minutes or until contents are bubbly and top is golden brown.

Serves 4

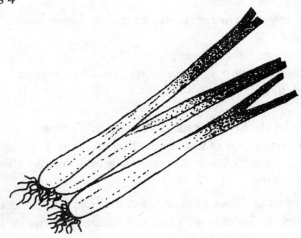

Chicken Paprika

There are many versions of this popular Hungarian goulash, but cooks agree that it must be made with imported Hungarian paprika.

4	fresh or frozen skinless, boneless chicken breast halves
	Salt and pepper
2	tablespoons vegetable oil
2	medium onions, chopped
3	tablespoons Hungarian paprika
1/2	teaspoon dried marjoram
1/8	teaspoon freshly grated nutmeg
2	bay leaves
1/8	teaspoon cayenne
1/2	cup tomato sauce
1/2	cup low-salt chicken broth, canned or homemade (page 177)
2	teaspoons fresh lemon juice
1/4	cup sour cream, or plain yogurt, lowfat or regular (optional)

1. For fresh chicken breasts, go to step 2. If breasts are frozen, place in a sealed plastic bag and thaw in a large pan of cold water for 25 to 30 minutes or until flexible. Blot with paper towels.

2. Trim fresh or thawed breasts of any visible fat. Cut into bite-size pieces. Sprinkle with salt and pepper. In a heavy, large saucepan or deep, large skillet, heat oil over medium heat. When oil shimmers, add chicken pieces. Cook, stirring, until no longer pink, 4 to 5 minutes. With a slotted spoon, remove chicken pieces to a bowl and set aside.

3. In the same pan, add onions and cook, stirring and scraping pan bottom to incorporate browned bits, until onions are golden brown. Add paprika, marjoram, nutmeg, bay, and cayenne. Stir to coat the onions with the spices. Add tomato sauce, broth, and lemon juice. Bring to a boil, then reduce heat to low, cover, and simmer until onions are tender, about 10 minutes. Return chicken to the pan with any accumulated juices from the dish. Cover and heat through, 4 to 5 minutes. Taste and add salt, if needed. Stir in sour cream, if desired. Do not allow goulash to boil after sour cream is added, or the sauce will curdle. Serve hot.

Serves 4

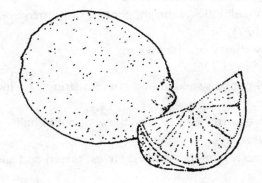

Philippine Chicken Apritada

*Felicia Garlitos, of San Francisco, California, contributed this
rustic chicken stew from the Philippines. It's delicious all by
itself, or you can serve it over rice, as Felicia suggests.*

3	fresh or frozen skinless, boneless chicken breast halves
	Salt and pepper
1	teaspoon plus 3 tablespoons olive oil
2	medium russet potatoes, peeled and cut into bite-size pieces
1	medium onion, sliced lengthwise
4	garlic cloves, chopped
4	roma tomatoes, peeled and coarsely chopped
1	can (8 ounces) tomato sauce
1/2	cup low-salt chicken broth, canned or homemade (page 177)
1/4	cup dry sherry or white wine
2	bay leaves
1	red bell pepper, seeded and cut into strips 1 1/2 inches by 1/4 inch
1	cup frozen artichoke hearts, thawed, cut in half lengthwise
8	to 10 green pimiento-stuffed olives, rinsed and sliced crosswise

1. For fresh chicken, go to step 2. If breasts are frozen, to
   thaw quickly, rinse under running water 3 to 5 minutes or
   until flexible. Blot with paper towels.

2. Trim fresh or thawed breasts of excess fat. Cut into 1-inch
   pieces. Pat dry, and sprinkle lightly with salt and pepper.
   Place chicken pieces in a medium bowl and toss, to coat

with 1 teaspoon oil to help prevent sticking to pan when cooking.

3. In a heavy, large saucepan or Dutch oven, heat 2 table-spoons of the oil over medium-high heat. When oil shimmers, add chicken and cook, stirring rapidly, until chicken is no longer pink, 4 to 5 minutes. With a slotted spoon, transfer to a bowl. Reduce heat to medium, add remaining 1 tablespoon oil, and cook potatoes, tossing, until golden, 4 to 5 minutes. Add onion, garlic, and tomatoes. Cook, stirring and scrapping pan bottom to loosen any browned particles, for 2 minutes. Add remaining ingredients, except the chicken. Bring contents to a boil, reduce heat to medium-low, cover, and cook, stirring frequently, until potatoes are tender, about 15 minutes. Return chicken to the pan, reduce heat to low, and simmer 5 minutes. Remove bay leaves. Serve hot.

Serves 4

Chicken Posole

New Mexican-style posole is a spicy meal in a bowl just right for those who like it hot. This modern version using chicken breasts is easy to prepare and low in fat. Pure New Mexico chili powder can be found in the Mexican section of most supermarkets or in Latin American food stores. New Mexico chiles can be very spicy, so start with the smaller amount. More can be added after tasting.

3	fresh or frozen skinless, boneless chicken breast halves
	Salt and pepper
4	cups low-salt chicken broth, canned or homemade (page 177)
2	tablespoons vegetable oil
1	large onion, chopped
3	large garlic cloves, chopped
1	to 3 tablespoons pure New Mexico chili powder
1 1/2	teaspoons dried oregano, crumbled
1 1/2	teaspoons ground cumin
2	cans (15 ounces each) white or yellow hominy, drained and rinsed
1	cup canned crushed tomatoes
	Shredded cabbage
	Diced avocado
	Fresh lime wedges
	Flour tortillas

1. For fresh chicken, go to step 2. If breasts are frozen, to thaw quickly, rinse under running water for 3 to 5 minutes or until flexible. Blot with paper towels.

2. Trim fresh or thawed chicken of any visible fat. Cut into 1-inch pieces and place in a medium saucepan. Sprinkle chicken lightly with salt and pepper. Add 2 cups of the chicken broth and bring to a boil over medium heat. Reduce heat to low, cover, and simmer until chicken pieces are no longer pink, about 5 minutes. Remove pan from heat and let chicken sit in broth.

3. In a heavy, large saucepan, heat oil over medium heat. Add onion and garlic. Cook, stirring, until softened, 3 to 4 minutes. Stir in chili powder, oregano, and cumin and cook about 30 seconds. Add remaining 2 cups of chicken broth, hominy, and tomatoes. Bring to a boil and cook over medium-low heat, covered, for about 10 minutes to blend flavors. Add chicken and broth in which it was cooked. Bring to a boil, then reduce heat to low, cover, and simmer until completely heated through, 2 to 3 minutes.

4. Serve posole in shallow soup plates, garnished with shredded cabbage and avocado. Pass lime wedges to squeeze over soup at the table. Place soft warm tortillas in a napkin-lined basket and put on the table.

Serves 4

Chicken, Onion, and Rice Casserole

This dish is similar to a French Soubise which is a slowly cooked mixture of onions, butter, and rice. The addition of chicken and cheese makes a satisfying whole meal casserole. Just add a crisp salad.

3	fresh or frozen skinless, boneless chicken breast halves
2	tablespoons unsalted butter
1	tablespoon vegetable oil
4	medium onions, coarsely chopped
1/2	cup long-grain rice
1	cup (4 ounces) shredded Swiss cheese
1 1/2	cups whole milk
	Salt and white pepper
1/4	cup bread crumbs
1	teaspoon olive oil
1/2	teaspoon paprika

1. For fresh chicken, go to step 2. If breasts are frozen, place in a sealed plastic bag and thaw in a large pan of cold water for 25 to 30 minutes or until flexible.

2. Trim fresh or thawed chicken breasts of any visible fat. Cut into 1/2-inch pieces. Place in a bowl and set aside.

3. Melt butter and oil in a large, deep skillet over medium heat. Add onions, stir to coat with butter, cover and reduce heat to medium-low. Cook, stirring occasionally, until softened, about 10 minutes. Do not brown the onions. Add chicken pieces and cook, stirring, until chicken is no longer pink, 3 to 4 minutes. Remove from heat and set aside.

4. Preheat oven to 350°. In a medium saucepan bring 2 cups water to boil. Add rice and boil 5 minutes, uncovered. Drain, but don't rinse, and stir into the onion mixture along with the cheese and milk. Season to taste with salt and white pepper. Turn into a 1¹/₂-quart buttered ovenproof baking dish.
5. In a small bowl, mix bread crumbs, olive oil, and paprika. Sprinkle crumbs over the casserole. Bake in preheated oven for about 35 minutes or until blade of sharp knife can easily pierce the onions. Serve hot.

Serves 4 to 6

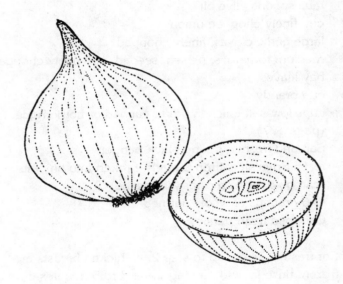

Spanish Chicken and Saffron Stew

Spain raises a large supply of the world's saffron and uses it in many inventive ways. Serve this fragrant chicken and saffron broth with steamed rice spooned right into the bowl. For an extra touch of Spain, offer good country bread and Mediterranean olives.

4	fresh or frozen skinless, boneless chicken breast halves
3	tablespoons olive oil
1/2	cup finely chopped onion
2	large garlic cloves, finely chopped
2	medium tomatoes, peeled, seeded, and finely chopped
2	bay leaves
1/3	cup brandy
1 1/3	cups low-salt chicken broth, canned or homemade (page 177)
	Salt and freshly ground black pepper
14	to 16 Spanish saffron threads, broken into tiny bits (can be done in mortar with pestle)
4	to 6 gratings of whole nutmeg
	Chopped fresh parsley

1. For fresh chicken, go to step 2. If chicken breasts are frozen, rinse in cold running water 3 to 5 minutes or until flexible. Blot with paper towels.

2. Trim fresh or thawed breasts of any visible fat and cut into neat 1-inch pieces. Cover and reserve on a plate, or refrigerate if done ahead.

3. In a heavy, medium skillet, heat oil over medium heat and sauté onion and garlic, stirring, until softened, about 3 minutes. Add remaining ingredients, except the chicken bits and parsley. Bring to a brisk boil. Reduce heat to medium-low, cover, and cook the broth for 5 minutes. (Can be prepared ahead to this point.)

4. Shortly before serving, bring sauce to a boil. Add the chicken pieces, reduce heat to low, cover, and cook until the chicken bits are just firm to the touch and no pink remains, 6 to 8 minutes. Divide equally among four shallow soup plates. Sprinkle with parsley, and serve hot.

Serves 4

Chicken Stew with Sun-Dried Tomatoes and Baby Lima Beans

A quick and healthy stew with great flavor in record time!

4	fresh or frozen skinless, boneless chicken breast halves
2	tablespoons flour
3	tablespoons olive oil
1	medium onion, halved and sliced
2	garlic cloves, finely chopped
1/2	cup dry white wine
3/4	cup low-salt chicken broth, canned or homemade (page 177)
1	package (10 ounces) frozen baby lima beans
1/4	cup chopped fully cooked smoked ham
6	to 8 oil-packed sun-dried tomatoes, slivered
1	tablespoon tomato paste
1	teaspoon dried marjoram leaves
1	teaspoon Worcestershire sauce
	Salt and pepper
3	tablespoons finely chopped fresh parsley

1. For fresh chicken, go to step 2. If chicken breasts are frozen, rinse under cold running water 3 to 5 minutes or until flexible. Blot with paper towels.

2. Cut fresh or thawed breasts into 1 1/2-inch pieces. Remove visible fat. Dust chicken pieces with flour. Shake off excess flour. In a large, heavy saucepan, heat 2 tablespoons of the oil over medium heat. Brown chicken pieces on both sides.

With slotted spoon, remove to a dish. Add remaining tablespoon oil to the pan and cook onion and garlic, stirring for
about 3 minutes or until onions are softened. Add wine and
chicken broth. Scrape bottom of pan to incorporate any
browned bits. Add lima beans, ham, tomatoes, tomato
paste, marjoram, and Worcestershire sauce. Bring to a boil,
then reduce heat to low and simmer 5 minutes, partially
covered. Return chicken to the pan. Season to taste with
salt and pepper. Cover and simmer 10 minutes. Stir in
parsley and serve.

Serves 4

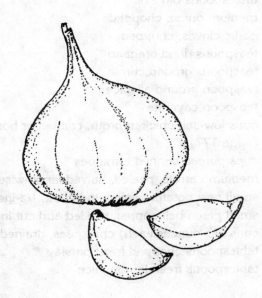

Turkish Chicken Stew
with Chickpeas

This aromatic and full-flavored stew was inspired by all the wonderful smells and tastes of a recent visit to Turkey.

3	fresh or frozen chicken breast halves
	Salt and pepper
2	tablespoons flour
3	tablespoons olive oil
1	medium onion, chopped
3	garlic cloves, chopped
1 1/2	teaspoons dried oregano
1 1/2	teaspoons ground cumin
1/2	teaspoon ground allspice
1/8	teaspoon cayenne
2	cups low-salt chicken broth, canned or homemade (page 177)
1 1/2	cups pureed canned tomatoes
2	medium carrots, peeled, halved lengthwise, and sliced
1	small new potato, peeled and cut in 1/2-inch cubes
1	small green bell pepper, seeded and cut in 1/2-inch cubes
2	cans (15 ounces each) chickpeas, drained and rinsed
2	tablespoons chopped fresh parsley
2	tablespoons fresh lemon juice

1. For fresh chicken, go to step 2. If chicken breasts are frozen, place in a sealed plastic bag and thaw in a large pan of cold water for about 30 minutes or until flexible. Blot with paper towels.

2. Trim any visible fat from fresh or thawed breasts and cut into 1-inch pieces. Sprinkle lightly with salt and pepper. Dust with flour, shaking off excess. In a heavy, large saucepan, heat oil over medium heat. When oil shimmers, add chicken pieces and cook, stirring, until no longer pink, about 4 minutes. With slotted spoon, remove chicken to a bowl. To the pan, add onion, garlic, oregano, cumin, all-spice, and cayenne. Cook, stirring and scraping bottom of pan to loosen any browned particles, until onion is translucent, 3 to 4 minutes. Add additional oil, if needed. Adjust heat to prevent burning. Add broth, tomatoes, carrots, potato, and green pepper. Bring to a boil, then reduce heat to medium-low, cover, and cook until vegetables are tender, 10 to 12 minutes.

3. Place 1 cup of the chickpeas in a small bowl and mash with a fork. Stir into the stew along with the rest of the chickpeas. Return chicken to the pan with any accumulated juices. Add parsley and lemon juice. Bring stew to a boil and simmer over low heat, uncovered, for 10 minutes. Taste and add salt and pepper, if needed.

Serves 4

Chicken and Vegetable Chowder

Chowders are nourishing make-ahead meals, and they reheat very well. This unconventional version is lush and satisfying.

3	fresh or frozen skinless, boneless chicken breast halves
3 1/2	cups low-salt chicken broth, canned or homemade (page 177)
2	tablespoons butter
1	tablespoon vegetable oil
1	medium onion, chopped
2	large garlic cloves, chopped
1	teaspoon dried oregano, crumbled
2	medium russet potatoes (about 1 pound), peeled and thinly sliced
1	can (5 1/3 ounces) evaporated milk
4	to 6 drops Tabasco sauce
2	medium zucchini, trimmed and coarsely shredded
1	medium carrot, peeled and coarsely shredded
1/2	red bell pepper, cut into 1/8 inch pieces
	Salt and freshly ground black pepper
4	slices crisp-fried bacon, crumbled into bits (optional)

1. If chicken is fresh, go to step 2. If breasts are frozen, to thaw quickly, rinse under cold running water for 3 to 5 minutes or until flexible.

2. Trim fresh or thawed breasts of any visible fat. Cut breasts into 2-inch pieces and place in a medium saucepan. Add 1 cup of the chicken broth and bring to a boil over medium-high heat. Reduce heat to low, cover, and simmer until no

longer pink, 4 to 5 minutes. Remove pan from heat, set aside, and let chicken cool in the broth.

3. In a large saucepan, heat butter and oil over medium heat. Add onion, garlic, and oregano. Cook, stirring frequently, until softened, 3 to 4 minutes. Add potatoes, remaining 2 1/2 cups chicken broth, evaporated milk, and Tabasco sauce. Bring to a boil over medium-high heat. Partially cover, reduce heat to medium-low, and cook until potatoes are very tender, 10 to 12 minutes. Puree soup in food processor or blender. Return soup to pan and bring to a boil over medium-high heat. Add zucchini, carrot, and red pepper. Cook over medium-low heat, stirring frequently, until vegetables are tender, 6 to 8 minutes. Remove chicken pieces from cooled broth and tear into coarse shreds. Add the shredded chicken to the soup. (Save broth from cooking chicken for another purpose, unless needed to thin the soup.) Cook soup over medium-low heat, stirring constantly to prevent sticking, until completely heated through, 4 to 5 minutes. Season to taste with salt and freshly ground black pepper. Sprinkle each serving with crisp bacon bits, if desired.

Serves 4

Chicken and White Bean Casserole in Spicy Tomato Sauce

A dependable casserole to prepare quickly for busy days or for a potluck supper.

4	fresh or frozen skinless, boneless chicken breast halves
	Salt and pepper
2	tablespoons olive oil
1/2	medium onion, chopped
2	garlic cloves, chopped
1	tablespoon chili powder
2	cans (15 ounces each) small white beans, drained but not rinsed
1	can (14 1/2 ounces) ready-cut salsa-style tomatoes
1	tablespoon prepared barbecue sauce
2	green onions, including 2 inches of green, chopped
2	jalapeño chiles, seeded and chopped
1	tablespoon red wine vinegar

1. For fresh chicken, go to step 2. If breasts are frozen, place in a sealed plastic bag and thaw in a large pan of cold water for 25 to 30 minutes or until flexible. Blot with paper towels.

2. Preheat oven to 350°. Trim fresh or thawed breasts of any visible fat. Cut each breast in half lengthwise. Sprinkle lightly with salt and pepper. In a large, nonstick skillet, heat oil over medium heat. Add chicken and cook until lightly browned, about 4 minutes. Turn and cook second side for 2

minutes. Remove chicken to a plate. (Chicken will not be cooked through.)

3. In the same skillet, cook onion and garlic, stirring, until softened, 3 to 4 minutes. Stir in chili powder. Add beans, tomatoes, barbecue sauce, green onions, jalapeños, and vinegar. Bring to a boil, then transfer to ovenproof casserole. Place chicken breasts on top of the beans and tuck into the sauce. Pour any accumulated juices over the breasts. Cover and bake until bubbling throughout and juices run clear when chicken is pierced in thickest part with tip of a sharp knife, 35 to 40 minutes.

Serves 4

Index